D1568691

COLOR IN ARCHITECTURE

Design Methods for Buildings,
Interiors, and Urban Spaces

Harold Linton

McGraw-Hill

New York   San Francisco   Washington, D.C.   Auckland   Bogotá
Caracas   Lisbon   London   Madrid   Mexico City   Milan
Montreal   New Delhi   San Juan   Singapore
Sydney   Tokyo   Toronto

McGraw-Hill

A Division of The **McGraw·Hill** *Companies*

Copyright © 1999 by the McGraw-Hill Companies, Inc. All rights reserved. Printed in the United Stated of America. Except as permitted under the United States Copyright Act of 1976, no part of this publication may be reproduced or distributed in any form or by any means, or stored in a data base or retrieval system, without the prior written permission of the publisher.

1 2 3 4 5 6 7 8 9 0 1IMP/1IMP 9 0 4 3 2 1 0 9

ISBN 0-07-038119-4

The sponsoring editor for this book was Wendy Lochner, and the production supervisor was Sherri Souffrance. It was set in Candida by North Market Street Graphics.

Printed in Hong Kong by Print Vision

McGraw-Hill books are available at special quantity discounts to use as premiums and sales promotions, or for use in corporate training programs. For more information, please write to Director of Special Sales, McGraw-Hill, 11 West 19th Street, New York, NY 10011. Or contact your local bookstore.

This book is dedicated to my children, Joshua and Jonathan, with wishes for all of the happiness and enjoyment that come from productive lives. Remember that fulfilled ambitions, hopes, and dreams come slowly from hard work. Always remain true to yourselves and to your belief in the right thing to do. I love you and wish you the world.

CONTENTS

FOREWORD

Color in Architecture: Design Methods for Buildings, Interiors, and Urban Spaces explores the most profound aspects of planning color for architecture and the allied disciplines. What the color design professional brings to the architectural design team is not only an expertise devoted to supporting the guiding design concept of a building, but also a richly diverse sensibility made up of broad awareness and a finely tuned visual perception. This includes a knowledge of design and its history, expertise with industrial color materials and their methods of application, an awareness of design context and cultural identity, a background in physiology and psychology as they relate to human welfare, and an ability to respond creatively to design concepts with innovative ideas for color, light, form, and space. Not only is the color designer responsive to all of the visual stimuli relating to architecture, the colorist is also aware of present and future color trends and materials and their potential influence on contemporary and historic structures. It is just such a broadening of the definition of the colorist's role in design that makes this book so relevant and significant to education and the profession of color design.

The role of the color designer striving to complete the work of the architect did not really appear until the 1950s, shortly after the end of the Second World War. Historically, in Europe, it was industrial architecture that made use of and supported the work of colorists. A little later, around 1960, the appearance of huge apartment complexes that tended to be somber and repetitive in appearance created the need to personalize these buildings with color.

In France, since about 1970, new multidisciplinary teams comprised of urban planners, architects, and colorists have come together to build new cities. As colorists sought to respond to the needs of various early programs, it became evident that they had found themselves in a new, experimental territory—and as yet there was no formal education or school for color as applied to

architecture. To find solutions, colorists and architects used different methods in ways that one could describe as fumbling and
speculative at first but which with experience became progres-
sively more concrete. This is one of the ways this book takes its
historic place.

In demonstrating, through many examples, the process of the
work of visual artists and designers, theoreticians, and those of a
more analytical and rational method, Harold Linton here once
again opens a new and essential chapter in his investigative work
on the practical role of color in landscape, architecture, and design
in our time. With many published works on various aspects of color,
including *Color Model Environments, Color in Architectural Illustration, Color Consulting,* and *Color Forecasting,* he has made
invaluable contributions toward shaping the future of color education and giving definition to color design professions. *Color in
Architecture; Design Methods for Buildings, Interiors, and Urban
Spaces* offers an in-depth look at the methods, materials, and especially the preliminary color design processes of many colleagues—
both architects and artists—who practice at the top of their
profession. Nothing like this has ever been attempted before, for
many reasons. Perhaps the most important of these reasons is the
fact that many designers feel protective, if not secretive, about sharing the most personal aspects and evidence of their color design
processes. But Linton's reputation in color education and the
respect he has amassed for being sensitive and innovative as an
educator and color professional make a work of this magnitude possible and intriguing as a resource for students and professionals.

I have known Linton's work for almost two decades and have
participated in various publishing projects and educational experiences with him. His most recent accomplishment, described in
the education chapter of this book, is the founding, with his col-
league Harald Arnkil, of the first masters of arts degree program
in color and design in Europe, at the University of Art and Design
(UIAH) in Helsinki, Finland. This graduate program is a milestone in the history of color education and marks the first
moment, since Josef Alber's color course at Yale in the 1950s, that

an academic institution of the arts has embarked on a course of color study so ambitious and dedicated exclusively to training students for color design in the fine and design arts. All of those involved in color and design throughout the world should feel a special bond to what has occurred in Helsinki, and to the ground-breaking work that has transpired. It will have long-lasting impact for our profession as it matures and grows into a vibrant research and creative entity for future color designers.

The work for this book began simultaneously with the work for the new M.A. degree program. Linton embarked on this project with the background thought in mind to share his understanding of the many methods of color design planning with his graduate students, which in turn would serve to illustrate the diversity of professional methods of color planning and varied aesthetics and preferences, as well as acquaint his students with an awareness of a sampling of some of the most well-known practitioners in the field of color today. With this work, he has pushed open the windows, eyes, hearts, and minds of design educators around the world. *Color in Architecture* is far more than a work about surface treatments for buildings. It is an in-depth reflection of the state of the profession as it relates to the built environment. Our legacy is reflected in the many examples gathered from countries throughout the world, including a diversity of cultures and attitudes regarding the palette and design and the uniqueness of geographical climate, light, and season, and human orientation to all of these factors.

Linton speaks from professional experience as a mature educator, professional artist, and color designer. His mission in education has been to build color awareness and simultaneously define the profession as a viable and fulfilling career path for students of architecture and the allied disciplines. This is why I celebrate Harold Linton's book as an outstanding effort to bring the importance of the color professional into proper perspective.

Jean-Philippe Lenclos
Atelier 3d Couleur
Paris, France

PREFACE

The purpose of this book is to demonstrate and discuss the methods of color planning and design for architecture, interiors, and urban spaces. It has been my objective in teaching advanced courses in color design in the United States and abroad to identify color design as an academic discipline related to architecture and also to help define the profession of color designer as a valued member of the architectural team. This book will relate significant design and industry precedents to a discussion of planning concepts of the visual and physical properties of color for architectural applications, and relate these aspects to an international survey of the work of accomplished, contemporary colorists whose comments regarding color methodologies in design, architecture, and art accompany their work.

The discussions and illustrations included are intended to provide the reader with insight into professional practice that distinguishes many color designers by bringing attention to their methods of uniting color and light with form and space in the design process. The images have been selected to demonstrate individual perceptions and studio methods of color planning leading to the design, selection, and application of color materials for architecture, interior, and urban design projects. The images also reflect a sampling of international practices in color design and of the rich variety of cultural, physical, geographical, and climatic elements affecting design professionals and their work. Images in series, details of larger works, and plans and visual documentation of building materials and construction processes are presented and accompanied by views of completed projects, allowing comparison from more than one context.

Recognizing the existence of a growing number of environmental color designers and an expanding interest in their profession, many educational institutions and professional organizations are

responding by identifying programs and courses in color education, along with capable personnel to carry out color work across a
broad range of activities with up-to-date methods and tools for an
ever-increasing array of clients. As one example, several institutions of higher education in the United States, including my own
in Michigan, have created advanced courses in color design
related directly to architecture and interior design, taught by
senior faculty with special interests in this area. Most recently, a
master's degree program in color design was begun at the University of Art and Design in Helsinki, Finland, dedicated solely to the
study and practice of color in art and architecture. The Color
Design Research Unit of South Bank University in London,
England, has also instituted a series of courses and seminars
specifically focused on color related to product development and
marketing across a broad range of design professions. The International Association of Color Consultants has a multifaceted,
interdisciplinary curriculum in color design with the aim of equip-
ping graduates with the broad palette of skills and perceptions
necessary to work efficiently in today's architectural and interior
design offices and allied industry disciplines. Several art institutions in Europe, the United States, and Australia now offer undergraduate and postgraduate interdisciplinary programs of two and
four years, variously called *color design, color communications,
color marketing,* and *color science,* which strive to equip their
graduates with a special depth of experience and knowledge to
pursue advanced color study and careers in design industries.
These programs and others are discussed in Part Eight of this
book.

I would like to extend my appreciation to my colleagues and
friends who have given freely of their time and advice to make
this publication possible. In particular these include Wendy Lochner, senior editor for architecture and design at McGraw-Hill Professional Books, New York; Jean-Philippe Lenclos and the staff of
Atelier 3d Couleur, Paris; and Maggie Toy, editor of architecture
and senior publishing editor at John Wiley & Sons, London. My

special thanks also go to translation specialist Galit Zolkower in Silver Spring, Maryland; to Julie Hoelscher of Farmington, Michigan, for graphic and manuscript development; and to the administration of Lawrence Technological University in Southfield, Michigan, for the generous support of a professional development leave of absence. Finally, my warm regards go to all of my colleagues who have contributed examples of their work for inclusion in this book.

INTRODUCTION

Color is an immensely evocative medium, possessing inherent
powers to provoke immediate and marked reactions in the viewer,
and as such it has been developed as a language of symbol in
both the natural and the man-made worlds. Its use in architecture
and the built environment is no exception, serving to dramatically
affect perception of architectural space and form.

However, when incorporated into this discipline color's highly
subjective nature is also emphasized. Until recently its use has
been one of the most unpredictable areas of architectural decoration; each individual's experiences differ, and no amount of analysis can successfully foretell how people will respond to the same
color. Almost any generalization that can be made about color can
be overturned in practice.

Perhaps the notion of a color continuum throughout periods of
architectural history from the Greeks to the present suggests the
continual human fascination with color and a natural process of
reinvention of color in architecture and the design environment.
Periods of high architectural coloration, such as today, have been
preceded (and followed) by periods of more neutral architectural
coloration. There is a band of architects whose work tends to be
termed "minimal"—a development from the Modern Movement
and International Style, which abhorred the use of applied decoration. The color scheme often associated with this type of design is
based on variations of white, which allows the colors and light in
the surrounding environment to reflect into the space: Thus the
design lives in its site. Perhaps this is the antithesis of the brightly
colored architecture featured in this book. And perhaps this
twentieth-century tradition/trend also goes some way toward
answering the question of why architectural education has rarely
focused on color and its effects. Color is often considered merely
as an afterthought, as the domain of the interior designer, cast out
with other forms of decoration by Modernists at the beginning of

the century. Le Corbusier followed Adolf Loos and echoed the feelings of many at the time when he declared that the more civilized societies used less applied decoration.

Mexican Luis Barragan has been the mentor for many architects keen to utilize color within their designs. Barragan's architecture catches wind and water more effectively than the ideas and anxieties of the moment, but its virtue lies in just that. Color is an essential dimension—as opposed to a mere decorative element—of his work. While many architects have been inspired by Barragan, the work of a group of California architects particularly echoes his color philosophy. Mark Mack never hesitates to use bold colors, sometimes with almost random distribution, though they are always matched with materials to give them true substance and identity. Ricardo Legorreta is also a wonderful example of a "color architect," who understands the effects that color can have on architectural planes. Color accentuates shape and yet can actively deny the real mass of a building form. Carrying forward the traditions of twentieth-century muralist painters, Legorreta spreads a rich work of art across entire walls, coloring them bright yellow, sky blue, or vivid magenta in apparent defiance of their massive reality. Strong statements of a proud architecture, they are not polemical but contemporary abstract art.

Such implementations of color do not exist only in bright locations. Even within the rainy bounds of London, architects CZWG persist in the use of bright colors in significant locations. Their public toilets, finished in bright turquoise tile, were built in West London, despite being in a strict conservation area and requiring the raising of extra money by the residents.

Perhaps it is necessary to have strict rules for the application of color in architecture. Angela Wright, color psychologist and author of *A Beginner's Guide to Colour Psychology* (published by Kyle Cathie, Ltd., London, 1995), argues that there are patterns which can be calculated so that, given a correct amount of information, the "correct" color combinations can be achieved in a scientific manner. Perhaps it is the lack of such guidance in architectural schools that has led to the lack of color in some areas—followed, with the onslaught of Postmodernism in the 1980s, by a flood of bizarre color arrangements. In 1856, Owen Jones, a British architect and author of *The Grammar of Ornament,* a highly influential nineteenth-century book of architectural decoration, set out a series of principles to be observed when using colors. These went right back to the basics and included explanations of the effects of color and instructions on where to place certain colors in relation to others. Jones felt that no improvement would take place unless principles were defined and adhered to and the public at large were better educated. Certainly a greater emphasis could be placed today on teaching the qualities of color in architectural schools.

In this book, Harold Linton offers an unusual opportunity for a behind-the-scenes view of how professional color consultants and designers apply their artistry to support the creative visions of architecture and allied disciplines. The contributors to this book are outstanding examples of colorists working today in architecture and the design environment. They have shared their experiences and visions of color design from the early stages of color ideation, collaboration, and planning processes through the development of their work into full-scale realizations with sophisticated industrial methods and color materials. Linton teaches color to architects and promotes the role of the architectural colorist, who has often come to this occupation through a varied and circuitous pathway of education and professional experiences in art, graphic design, interior design, and architecture, and who lends a vital skill to the design team in all aspects of environmental design. He focuses attention on a full range of attributes of color design processes—from the creative and conceptual beginnings to planning methods, studio materials and media, graphic and three-dimensional model representations, computer realizations, industrial materials and their applications, professional contracts and agreements, and much more.

Throughout his professional life, Professor Harold Linton has supported the development of the colorist's profession. His many publications devoted to helping define the role of the color consultant, color forecaster, and color designer; his own professional work as an artist and color consultant; his teaching of specialized courses in environmental color design in Michigan and lectures in the United States and Europe; and most recently, his leadership in coestablishing the first master of arts degree program in color and design in Europe, at the University of Art and Design in Helsinki, Finland, continue to influence more and more generations of designers.

The selection of work from significant international color designers included in this volume covers all areas of environmental color design and will encourage all those who have an input into the design process to readdress the psychological effect of colors chosen for each and every element.

Maggie Toy
Editor of Architecture and Senior Publishing Editor,
John Wiley & Sons, London

COLOR IN
ARCHITECTURE

PART I

Color Styling
for Residential Architecture

Although architectural colors are often based on
building materials, it is the designer's use of
color, based on human understanding, that
enhances, emphasizes, and distinguishes architectural form and context in primary ways.
Specifying architectural color for residential
architecture requires the creation of a special
palette to anchor the structure and assist the
client in perceiving the building inside and out.

Studio materials and paint colors. (Photo: Tony Gunn.)

Concept, Materials, and Context

Color always has to have a context. What do the clients want to see when they come home? Do they want their building to blend into the environment, or to jump out from the streetscape, or to create a sense of excitement and anticipation as they arrive at the front door?

Australian color consultant Eva Fay, in collaboration with the Australian architectural firm Walton and Associates and project architect Kerry McGrath, has done a remarkable job in creating a distinctive coloration for a harborside residence. Perched high on a hill nestling in a background of native Sydney bushland, this home overlooks an arm of Sydney harbor. It is located in a suburb zoned mixed/heritage; how-

Exterior street facade. (Courtesy of *Australian House and Garden*. Photo: Tony Gunn.)

The starting point: Sydney sandstone, Homestead Red metal roofing, and aluminum window frames with powdercoat color of Moss Vale Sands. (Photo: Tony Gunn.)

"Color feeds us emotionally; it is not just aesthetic. Every color creates a mood. We all need all colors at different stages of our life, and my part is to determine the color needs for my clients within their environment. It is often necessary to take the client on a journey of color education. Color should just grab you and have the effect of "Wow!"—creating surprise and excitement, shock and suggestion."

Eva Fay
Rushcutters Bay, Australia

ever, council approval for color was not required.

The involvement of Eva Fay Colour Design began after the building frame was constructed and the building materials had been selected by the architect. Several key color elements, therefore, were already established. The roof was to be Homestead Red; the powdercoat color of the window and door frames was a pale, almost neutral color with a faint hint of olive green; and Sydney sandstone would clad the lower front section.

Eva Fay believes that color should be appropriate to the architecture and work in harmony with the architect's design. This building is about strong angular shapes, and strong angular form demands bold color design. Pastels would have been totally inappropriate.

The color planning process included several meetings with the client and architect, and various site visits to check the aspect, size, and proportions of walls and building areas to be colored, the local environmental coloration (natural and man-made), neighbors' house colors, and natural light levels. Eva then photo-documented the building structure, the adjoining streetscape, and environmental coloration for reference while working in the studio. From this point of departure, a strong ocher color immediately came to mind to work in harmony with the sandstone. The whole building could have been ocher, or even an interplay of ochers, but this would not have emphasized the cuboid design of Walton and Associates. The decision was made to color the walls with a cement-based (Murobond) finish coating, which creates

The selection of terra-cottas, ochers, and neutral colors from which Eva Fay chose one of each color. (Photo: Tony Gunn.)

Testing paint colors on-site. (Photo: Tony Gunn.)

a subtle, mottled variation or patina rather than a flat finish of acrylic paint.

Eva began working on the exterior color design with paper color swatches, putting together different combinations of hues and changing and adjusting their nuances to achieve the best interaction. The wall cladding of the two cubes facing the street presented large areas to be painted. A deep terra-cotta color seemed the best choice to interact with the ocher color. Several terra-cotta colors were paint-tested on the building, including one more bluish and the other more yellowish, to see the color effect in situ. For the third cuboid form, which is only seen from the side aspect of the residence, Eva wanted a neutral color to act as a foil for the ocher and the terra-cotta. A string-type color was chosen, a slightly deeper version of the window frame color.

The whole building was tied together by a prominent external steel structure. The color for

Complete colors for exterior.
(Photo: Tony Gunn.)

this material needed to be dark and bold, and to work together with the ocher and terra-cotta, and also not be too chromatic. Eva first considered a bluish charcoal color, because she wanted to link the steel structure with the bluish red of the roof; however she decided that she wanted something slightly more chromatic.

The selection of a deep, rich blue-purple that was slightly muted or grayed (eggplant color) was made to offset all the other colors. This eggplant color was not only on the steel structure but all the handrails and balustrades, and it also created a bold statement on the front door.

Color is all about what to focus on and where one wishes to direct the viewer's eye. It includes the process of layering, to determine what will advance or recede visually, as the colorist decides which architectural forms will be prominent and which will harmonize, blend, recede, or become camouflaged. Working as a color consultant constantly requires switching from working as designer on the project to working as an artist on the project, and vice versa. The challenge is in knowing how to paint a piece of sculpture, that is, the building, in three-dimensional color in context.

This synergy happens once all the information and criteria for the project are gathered; then an image is slowly developed, with much visualization and testing, to reach the end result in three-dimensional color; and the vision is communicated to the client. Color is not just an aesthetic; it feeds us emotionally. The colorist interprets people's color needs and emotions, and every color creates a mood. With the front door and entrance hall, for example, one hopes to create a sense of surprise, excitement, and a welcoming effect. As entry foyers/hallways are transition zones, colors can be quite strong without becoming overpowering, and in that instant of arrival and first sighting, the color effect sets the mood for the house.

Interior: Nature and Color-Space

The interior coloration was dictated by the aspect of each area, the size and proportion of the space, the degree of natural light, the client's color needs, the function of the space, and the architect's design concept.

The dominant flooring material for the living areas was to be rich polished timber, while the sleeping quarters had a mid-cornflower blue carpet. The kitchen/family zone would be a marmoleum of "broken" greens. Thus the tim-

Entry foyer. (Courtesy of *Australian House and Garden*. Photo: Russell Brooks.)

Bedroom colors. (Photo: Tony Gunn.)

ber floor created a warm hue, and as most areas had plenty of natural light with large glass windows, Eva used a very subtle cool off-white with a hint of olive green (Dulux Antarctic Ice) as the major wall and woodwork color. This cool neutral allowed the use of feature walls.

Eva believes in bringing the coloration of the exterior into the interior, thus creating a visual link and sense of belonging and anchoring. She brought the blue-purple color of the external balustrades inside to use on the staircase balustrade. The ocher cube cuts into the central glass core with a diagonal wall in the entry foyer, so the ocher coloring was also continued on this wall. On the opposite wall, Eva counterchanged the string color with a deep indigo blue to complement the blue from the carpet; this blade of color ran the full height of the stairwell, and thus was visible from the top level, with its views of Sydney harbor and all its blues, as well as from the foyer. The neutral color was the dominant wall and trim color throughout, allowing the natural materials (e.g., glass wall, timber, stainless steel) to become the focus and the accent wall colors to create surprise and visual flow. Two bedrooms are a play on blues, and the third one is tone-on-tone, with soft yellows.

Upstairs in the living area one looks out through a cutout section of the deep blue wall to

Dining area—terra-cotta wall. (Photo: Patrick Bingham Hall).

Kitchen—breakfast area. (Courtesy of *Australian House and Garden*. Photo: Russell Brooks.)

the low ocher walls of the balcony and the blue-green of the sea beyond, or else one can move through a large archway into the dining area, where a blade of terra-cotta color is juxtaposed against the end wall of deep blue-green.

In the kitchen and breakfast zone, which overlook the living area, the materials are both the focal point and the feature. A blackish green benchtop contrasts with a stainless steel bench-top; the cabinetry is a mid-tone timber; and the floor is a marmoleum of mottled greens and blue-greens. Eva highlighted the archway in a mid-green to frame the kitchen and relate to the floor and granite coloration.

Eva Fay thoroughly enjoys working with color because the process is never a constant and because a color's appearance always depends upon what it's juxtaposed with, leading to a dynamic experience in space and time.

Front facade in terra-cotta with blue-green and cream-colored details. (Photo: M. A. Grau.)

Historic Interest

In 1995, Malvina Arrarte Grau, architect, landscape designer, and colorist from Lima, Peru, was commissioned to work on the conversion of a nineteenth-century house to be turned into a day-care center. As the building was located in an area of historical interest in the Barranco district of Lima, it was important to maintain its architectural character. After an expensive reconstruction phase, paint and color became a main part of the job in achieving simple and economical finishes. The color choice for the facade was terra-cotta, a traditional color in Barranco. Blue-green was used as a contrasting tone for the woodwork, and cream for highlighting architectural elements. For operative reasons latex-based paint was used on the adobe walls instead of the traditional chalk and mineral pigment mixture. The floor plan shows the front and back courtyards, a corridor along the side, and the main body of the house. The latter is formed by

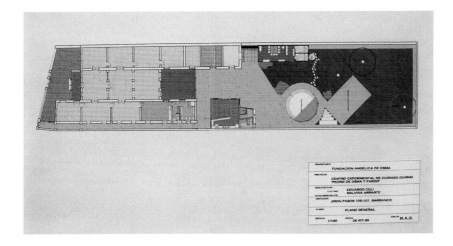

Floor plan of front and back courtyards. (Photo: M. A. Grau.)

three parallel rows of rooms, lit through the ceiling and perforated by doors and windows. Bright yellow was used for the main play space. The low levels of natural light suggested a triad of pastels for walls and plaster decorations. These would combine with blue-green windows and the terra-cotta and cream floor tiles. To complete the scheme the dado was painted in grayish-green enamel for visual weight and convenience in cleaning. The color scheme for the new dining

Main play space. (Photo: M. A. Grau.)

Color scheme for dining room.
(Photo: M. A. Grau.)

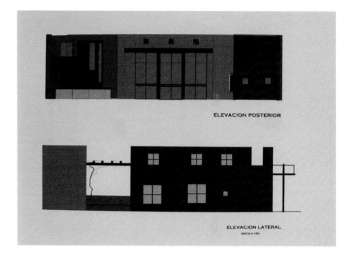

Back courtyard elevation. (Photo: M. A. Grau.)

"Balance is my standpoint in designing with color. Known harmonies work as a reference, but only after a thorough analysis a composition takes shape. I look for a correspondence between color and object. For understanding what the building (or setting) "wants to be," physical characteristics, context, and function are considered. Weathering is important, so the color range also depends on investment and maintenance decisions. Then comes color precision: experimenting with the actual materials, for colors should feel inherent to architecture at all possible scales."

Malvina Arrarte Grau
Lima, Peru

room was based on a triad of primary colors. This is shown with the colors of the facade and the glass blocks in the new courtyard elevation for a visualization of the whole scheme.

The new use of the building would probably suggest bright and contrasting colors. But in this case the scarce natural light coming from roof lanterns, the sequences of tightly interconnected spaces, and the plaster ornaments demanded a delicate use of color. A computer-drawn elevation shows the color proposal for the back courtyard. Bright blue was used to differentiate the dining-room exterior. The function of the rooms required distinctive atmospheres for sleeping, passive recreation, active recreation, newborn children, and so forth. The facade composition and the colors available for tiles and glass blocks also dictated the possibilities of the scheme. A corridor provides communication between the street and the back courtyard. For this forty-meter-long route, a mural painting was designed under given color parameters: Light blue should blend in with the sky of the created landscape to be seen from the windows.

Mural painting in corridor. (Photo: M. A. Grau.)

Computer image of Las Tres Marias
Condominium. (Photo: M. A. Grau.)

Image and Functionality

Las Tres Marias Condominium was a 1980s residential project for Lima, Peru, which existed
only on paper. It required changes in image
and functionality, in order to work for the target clients. Malvina Grau was asked to modify
the plans, keeping in mind warm and elegant
colors that would help to sell the houses. She
had the opportunity to give an original color
design proposal within economic and practical
limitations established by the real estate company. A three-dimensional image of a house
rendered in terra-cotta color was presented on
the first page of the brochure. It was important
that the color feel appropriate for the location
(which was sun-exposed and dusty) and that it
match the finishes. In the 14-family condo-

Condominium house plans.
(Photo: M. A. Grau.)

minium there were 4 different house plans. The location maps, floor plans, and colored elevations were shown in the brochure. Colors served to strengthen the character of the project and differentiate the houses from each other. "Floating walls" were designed as elements isolated from the continuity of the structure. The interiors received a general color, a warm off-white, while the floating walls could be painted as desired. Close coordination with the contractor and salesperson was crucial to

Paint tests on interior walls.
(Photo: M. A. Grau.)

Commercial palettes and computer-mixed
selections. (Photo: M. A. Grau.)

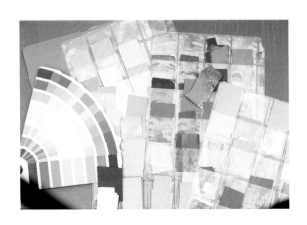

make the project work as a business. The color range offered to the clients was a selection from the commercial palette and latex samples mixed and tested by Malvina Grau. The paint was computer-mixed at the shop, including the special samples, which were codified by the computer. Colors were shown to the potential clients in computer-generated images made for a sales brochure. Medium-intensity earthly colors were chosen to feel homelike and to soften the shadows at different times of the day. A sequence of five houses seen from the access road to the condominium shows the preference for natural earthy colors for residential use in Lima in 1995. Most of the houses were sold soon after the first two units were painted. The color selection process was simple, and it proved efficient both as a marketing tool and as a means of identity.

Exterior view of painted condominiums. (Photo: M. A. Grau.)

Exterior view of several painted houses. (Photo: M. A. Grau.)

"For an architectural or industrial product purpose, the study of color requires the consultant to perform incessant repetitions. It means re-creating the life of an object no matter its scale. To create combinations of contrast in order to create visual and sensory emotions with color—with new objectives being provoked by communication needs: to give an impression of freshness, smell, warmth, exoticism, comfort. . . ."

Jean-Philippe Lenclos
Paris, France

Identity

The work of Jean-Philippe Lenclos has for many years been in the forefront of European and Japanese color design and touches nearly every design-related discipline, including architecture, interiors, fashion, graphics, products, advertising, fine arts, painting, and education. His studio in Paris, Atelier 3d Couleur, has been involved in architectural forecasting and controlling color trends.

Lenclos was the first designer to treat color as an independent element existing according to rules of nature, and the first to give color an identity connected with our daily lives. These ideas are contained in his early research. *Colors of France—Architecture and Landscape*, published in 1982, which includes studies of regional soil colors in France, provides color identity design concepts that proved useful for architectural colorations throughout the country.

Lenclos' work in analyzing various regions of France with the aim of identifying predominating chromatic characteristics began in the 1960s with his work as art director of the Societé des Peintures Gauthier, a French company producing industrial paints. Along with creating the company logo, color charts, graphics, and packaging, he directed his color expertise toward the various regions of France, where there is an extreme diversity of climates, from Mediterranean to Nordic, and a corresponding variety of building materials adapted to the local weather conditions. Lenclos analyzes this relationship of region, color, and building material by observing:

"The subject of architectural color in the modern landscape is essentially concerned with the visual quality of architecture, whether the environment be natural, urban, or industrial. Although a building may reflect the same range of colors as its mineral environment, its color is not static. It evolves, shifts, and changes seasonally as a result of changes in light, air, humidity, rain, and drought."

Lenclos' investigation essentially consists of assembling the existing architectural spectrum of an area or site, based on a systematic evaluation of the component elements and materials of a building.

Overall design of the layout of the 7 apartment buildings. (Photo: Jean-Philippe Lenclos.)

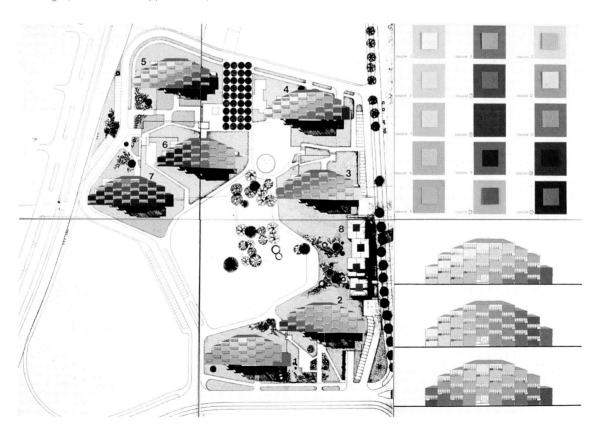

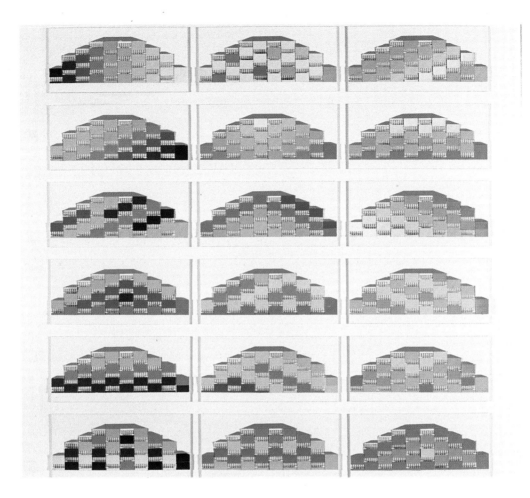

Rhythmic variants of a 15-color general palette.
(Photo: Jean-Philippe Lenclos.)

Phase One: Methodical Examination of the Sites

One method at this initial stage of the study is to rely, as far as possible, on the objective evidence provided by the architecture and its environment. Basically, this involves taking samples directly from the selected areas. The colorist methodically collects samples of materials and paint from the earth, walls, roofs, doors, shutters, etc., together with other natural substances such as moss and lichen. If a sample is impossible to obtain, a painted color match is made on the spot.

Phase Two: Synthesis of Collected Data

A long and meticulous process of synthesis now begins in the studio. All the collected samples are examined and translated into painted color plates which faithfully reproduce the original colors. The color plates are then classified and regrouped into panels which produce a color synthesis of both a region and of its architectural elements.

Phase Three: A System of Chromatic Conceptualization

The result of the field study and studio synthesis is the presentation of an applied color vocabulary appropriate to each of the regions of France. Two color programs are evolved, which are coordinated so that they can combine to

A palette of 15 dominant colors, along with 15 secondary colors. Rhythmic variations of colors on three facades. (Photo: Jean-Philippe Lenclos.)

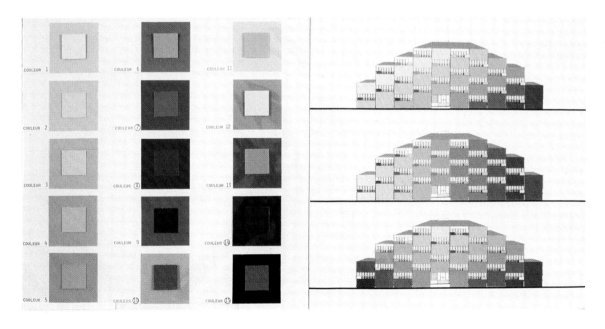

The apartment buildings have unique identities due to the varying rhythms in the color palettes chosen for each building. (Photo: Jean-Philippe Lenclos.)

offer harmony and variety in their application to existing or proposed future building projects.

Lenclos also observes, "Color in modern architecture can, therefore, be combined in new terms: The simultaneous construction of large-scale complexes which, being out of context with nature, create new urban landscapes. Two specific kinds of landscape emerge: the urban complex (housing, etc.) and the industrial zones." With high-rise buildings, Lenclos feels that color in material, structure, rhythm, and contrast can be a new plastic language whose powers of expression are able to add a poetic dimension which complements the man-made environment.

The housing ensemble at Chateau-Double, built in the Paris suburb of Aix-en-Provence by the architects Siame & Besson, was colored by Jean-Philippe Lenclos and is an excellent exam-

The apartment buildings' color identity is based on a clear plan for color values from light to dark. (Photo: Jean-Philippe Lenclos.)

ple of both a synthesis of color for the region and a successful palette for an urban context high-rise apartment complex. A general color design and concept was required for this group of 250 apartments in 7 identical buildings. Each apartment has a large terrace which serves to extend the living area to the exterior. The shape of the building is pyramidal. The overall color palette was chosen from within a range of 15 descending shades of ocher, beginning with a tone that is almost white, moving through tones of yellow, orange, and pink ocher, and ending with red ocher. The rhythmic movement of color values is what gives each building its own identity. Ultimately, the context of the building's scale and how color is successfully used to help shape a perception of the building in human scale added to the success of this project.

PART II

Interior Space Colorations

The reinvigoration of architecture through the decorative arts is a feature of contemporary interiors. The use of historical forms and symbols, the reintroduction of natural materials, and the influence of geographical location and climatic characteristics—including local color and light— are all determinants of the spatial perception of colors.

Period Color

Donald Kaufman, termed "America's Master Colorist" by *Connoisseur* magazine, and his partner, Taffy Dahl, believe that the rooms we live in can be colored to produce the same enriching atmosphere that we experience in nature. Employing some of the same traditional techniques that artists have used over the centuries, these colorists bring the harmony and variety of natural color indoors, creating hues with depth and luminosity. Their recent book, *Color: Natural Palettes for Painted Rooms,* is a beautifully illustrated publication that demonstrates rooms in which color creates rich and complex atmospheres. Whether the spaces are seemingly monochromatic or multihued, each room achieves its success through the use of palettes that are balanced across the spectrum. And though the subtleties of each surface cannot be captured exactly in photographs, many of the paints themselves contain a full spectrum of colorants. Kaufman and Dahl give thorough discussion to the method of mixing pigments in a paint-mixing guide at the close of their book, with advice regarding the formulation of one's own colors; suggestions on how to begin mixing your own paints; the appropriate ingredients and proportions; testing your results; working with a paint dealer; and altering commercial colors. During their professional careers, Kaufman and Dahl have developed color schemes for private residences, major museums, art galleries, and public spaces. Their work with architects and designers has included collaborations with Philip Johnson, Charles Gwathmey, Andre

"My wife, Taffy Dahl, and I work together as a check on each other's predilections and preconceptions. We try to understand the givens, and possible materials, in their most specific aspects. For example, what are the colors of the minute veins in the wood, or the barely visible particles in the stone, that add up to the perceived color? The Design Exchange project was successful because it was a broad collaboration in which the client [provided enough] time and money to be thorough and specific."

Donald Kaufman
New York, New York

Putman, Philippe Starck, and Pei, Cobb, Freed & Partners.

Working with the firm of Kuwabara Payne McKenne Blumberg architects, Donald Kaufman Color was asked to collaborate on the historic transformation of the Toronto, Ontario, Design Exchange (formerly the 1937 Toronto Stock Exchange) into a home for Canada's Design Directory, a comprehensive database of all post-war design in the nation and an exhibition hall which encourages design innovation of all kinds.

Better known as the D/X, the Design Exchange promotes Canada's industrial competitiveness by encouraging design innovation through exhibitions of the latest developments in consumer and industrial products, graphics, entertainment, fashion, architecture, landscaping, engineering, and city planning. A permanent location in the heart of Toronto's financial district assures the Exchange of maximum exposure to corporate leaders passing by as well as to its core membership of designers.

Serving on a rather elaborate design team with two architectural firms and many consultants, Donald Kaufman was asked to respond to the overall language of the original architecture, Art Modern, in a palette of understated hues for walls, ceilings, and architectural details that would serve to simplify and carry the design language throughout the four-story building and all of its various spaces and functions. A scheme of bold linear interventions comprising walls, ceiling planes, and stairs defines the public route through the spaces and creates a distinct architectural presence for the D/X. The material

The trading room, including murals by Charles Comfort. (Photo: Steven Evans.)

palette is also understated but bold, being comprised of stone, sandblasted crystal glass, and stainless steel—materials common to both heritage and contemporary structures. The color scheme of chartreuse, ocher, and azure is inspired by the restored Charles Comfort murals on the trading floor and featured in each space of the D/X.

Materials in the trading room include large sheets of etched glass along the bridge, while stainless steel handrails and oak flooring carry through the design intent of the original room. (Photo: Steven Evans.)

Graphite paint on the inside of the curtain-wall framing in the office building portion of the D/X echoes that on the exterior of this recent structure. (Photo: Steven Evans.)

Extra concrete beefs up the appearance of skinny support columns in the ground floor entrance hall but stays away from the ceiling to reveal the true structure. (Photo: Steven Evans.)

The resource center, which now serves small social functions, is reached by stairs directly from the trading room floor. (Photo: Steven Evans.)

Color Programming and Visibility

Shashi Caan is an associate and senior designer at Gensler Associates Architects in New York and serves as faculty trustee of the New York School of Interior Design. She is a highly creative and sensitive colorist who believes in the thorough exploration and visual analysis of the environment. Her recent work at Gensler for Fidelity Investments in New York City demonstrates this keen sensibility of observation, color planning, and creative vision.

The premise of the design is the need to provide a high-profile space in a highly visible location that maximizes customer draw, highlights the presence of Fidelity on Sixth Avenue, and serves as the company's flagship customer service center. An important and integral part of the design is about providing a sensory supportive and stimulating space through an innovative use of color.

Process

After formulating the client's needs (program) and identifying a site (building or space), these two need to be fitted together carefully. In this rational process, often called "space planning," the design aspect (i.e., the creation of sensory stimulating and supportive spaces) is not always fully appreciated or easily expressed. Particularly the unique opportunities that color offers to contribute to design are neglected or, worse, completely overlooked.

To avoid such omissions (and rather than starting from the inside out, and maybe adding

"If seeing color is about the translation of a three-dimensional phenomena into a sensory experience, then design must be about the transformation of aspects of sensory stimulation into three-dimensional color phenomena."

Shashi Caan
New York, New York

Exterior context of Fidelity Investments Customer Service Center, New York City. A collage of photographic images records the colors, textures, and light conditions of the unique corner site as well as the intermediate surroundings. This type of visual recording is essential in providing color information critical to the design process. The site is entered from the side street, with the long side of the two-story volume facing Sixth Avenue. With its corner location and Radio City Music Hall just across the street, the site has great visibility, suitable to a retail-type facility.
(Photo: Shashi Caan.)

color after the fact), the project was started from the outside in. A photographic collage of the surrounding area was assembled to establish a visual and color context for the design. In a manner similar to the formulation of a space program, a visually stimulating and sensory color program is created for the design by extrapolation out of the contextual photography.

Project Description

Fidelity Investments is located in 8000 square feet of space along Sixth Avenue, directly across the street from Radio City Music Hall. The site is a prominent, double-height retail space in the corner of the Time-Life Building. The entire space is fully visible from the Avenue, though a large fountain is located in the plaza directly in front. The actual entrance is on the short side of the long narrow space occupied by three large building columns. A large circular staircase providing access to the mezzanine level already existed at the other end of the space directly opposite the entrance. The stairs and mezzanine level were both retained but substantially redesigned.

Plan of Fidelity Investments Customer Service Center. The L-shaped space required articulation and the development of a hierarchy between the north-south direction and the lesser east-west axis. The three existing building structural columns did not align with the exterior wall. The other existing architectural elements consisted out of the two entrances (one from the street, the other from the building lobby) and a mezzanine and large circular staircase. A simple yet elegant design solution was conceived that allowed both the symmetry and the asymmetry to interact and generate both formality and dynamic motion. By taking a line from the main entrance through the center of the spiral stair and another one from the secondary entrance towards the front of the building the desired hierarchy is established. The east-west axis is very rectangular and forms a minor volume, while the dominant north-south axis is accentuated by pulling the columns out into the space. The intersection of the different axes is also reflected in the floor treatment. The lack of alignment of the building columns is no longer visible but has become an integral part of the design statement. The large vertical planes begin to interact with the front and back walls, creating a monolithic plane when seen from the main entrance. (Photo: Shashi Caan.)

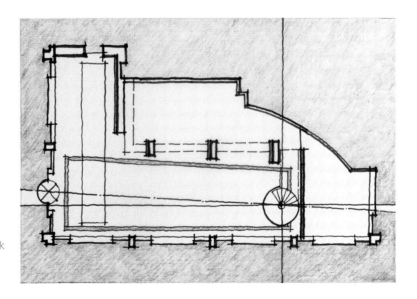

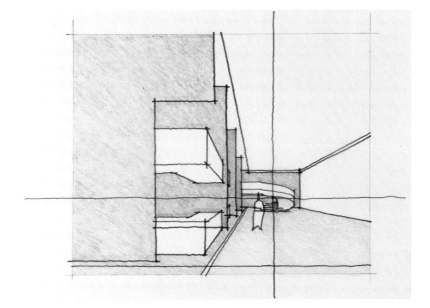

Partial perspective (from entrance) of Fidelity Investments Customer Service Center. The volume of the space is enhanced through a deliberate play with the perceptions of solid and void. Using a strong warm color (burnished copper), the planes of the columns and the walls in the north-south direction present a monolithic (solid) appearance, while in the perpendicular direction the volume is opened up (void). The solid color of the back wall also delineates the strong lines of the spiral staircase. (Photo: Shashi Caan.)

Sketch model (facing northwest) of Fidelity Investments Customer Service Center. The small-scale sketch model was used to explore the perceptions of solid and void and their interactions with strong colors, as well as the subtlety of the regular and irregular volumes, in creating the Renaissance notion of forced perspective. The latter emphasizes the volume and length of the space and allows for the masking of the irregularity of the column alignment. (Photo: Shashi Caan.)

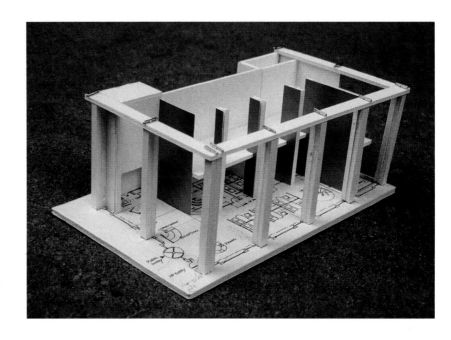

The three existing building columns have been used as an essential design element. By enlarging the column enclosures to different sizes, a series of large and overlapping vertical planes was created. Visually, when entering the space, these planes appear to be monolithic; however, when seen from the side the columns seem to be very narrow, which allows the space to be open and visually accessible. Because the column enclosures increase in size toward the back, the resulting tapering effect creates a forced perspective that enhances the illusion of

Design development model (facing northwest) of Fidelity Investments Customer Service Center. (Photo: Shashi Caan.)

Design development model (facing north) of Fidelity Investments Customer Service Center. The design development model allowed for further exploration of color and solid versus void. The colors were thereby refined with regard to values and hues to reinforce the overall design concept. (Photo: Shashi Caan.)

depth in the space. A narrow line of black marble inserted into the existing medium-gray granite floor further supports the enhanced perspective. The wide vertical planes of the column enclosures, the back wall of the space, and the wall in the front masking the service counter all have a burnished copper encaustic paint finish that is in clear contrast to the shiny stainless steel finish of the exterior curtain wall detailing.

The lighting of these vertical planes creates a very distinctive "glow" in the evening that enhances the overall visual intent. In addition to task and other more functional lighting, a large pendant fixture is located in the front of the space, at the intersection of the main space and

Design development model (facing west) of
Fidelity Investments Customer Service Center. The
two model views illustrate the color interaction
between the inside (new design) and the outside
(existing). Note the relative formality of the more
symmetrical treatment of the exterior, versus
the less formal and asymmetrical solution of the
interior. In addition, the color palette of the
exterior with its cool values (stainless steel and
glass) expresses that same formality, while the
warmer hues of the interior treatments enhance
the warmer and less formal solution of the inside.
(Photo: Shashi Caan.)

a small side space. This fixture, inspired by the
Fidelity logo, is intended to mark the entrance.
The intersection is further defined by the floor
pattern.

In addition to the service counters and other
back-of-house spaces, located under the mezzanine, the ground floor has a conference room
and open workstations. Additional offices
occupy portions of the mezzanine level.

The desired ambiance and the resulting colors and textures were established early in the

Color and material palette for Fidelity Investments Customer Service Center. The basic color and material palette makes use of mixed metals (stainless steel and brass) to establish a visual connection between the outside and the inside, as well as other materials such as wood and paint to introduce the necessary warm tones and create a sense of lightness. (Photo: Shashi Caan.)

design process as part of the contextual studies. Although the color of the context is largely cool, with neutral values ranging from medium to dark, the new colors and textures have been kept light in value, with strong warm tones for enhanced contrast. Three values have been used to give visual balance and human comfort: light (ceilings and walls), medium (only intense

Interior view from main entrance (facing north) of Fidelity Investments Customer Service Center. This view shows the large vertical planes of the columns, and the front and back walls with their copper color. The forced perspective gives the space the illusion of a larger depth than actually exists. The tracery of the 'mixed' metal handrail of the spiral stairs and mezzanine railing is clearly outlined against the back wall. (Photo: P. Ennis.)

Exterior night view (facing west) of Fidelity Investments Customer Service Center. The exterior night view shows the open character of the interior. More important, the dramatic quality of the glowing and white theatrical light in the interior draws attention to the space because of its direct contrast to the warmer light of Radio City Music Hall directly across the street. (Photo: P. Ennis.)

hue for the accent walls), and dark for the floor. The general visual texture appears to be small (windows, etc.) due to the massive scale of the streetscape and other high-rise architecture. The texture of the new materials is also kept simple and bold, again for deliberate contrast and scale with the surroundings.

Color Metaphor

Spain may be considered a sample of different geographic types, due to the diversity of its landscape and its different chromatic cultures. Villages in northern Spain, where cold, gray tones darken all the colors, are considerably different from the villages of Andalucia and Levante in the south and east, where white light produces greater chromatic contrasts. The popular Spanish architecture, designed and constructed by farmers and fishermen to respond to utilitarian demands, has become identified with the culture of each locale due to the use of indigenous building materials and the consistent adaptation of color to the local geography and climate.

Popular architecture for new rural locations, designed by professionals from their urban offices, continues to encroach upon the Spanish countryside villages with interventions, disrespective of even traditionally popular kitsch that in the south of Spain appeals to tourists.

The interior color artistry of Begona Munoz seeks to establish a careful, emotional interactive use of light and color, in a way as subtle and changing as occurs in nature. Looking for solutions that can satisfy the aesthetic feeling and physical welfare of people, she employs a broad, comprehensive understanding of cultural identity, interaction of light and pigment, and perception and psychology in the planning of each project. Her philosophy is reflected in the creation of the Musaeum Cafe Bar.

The space for the Cafe Bar was located on the ground floor of an old building that had been

Color in the common vestibule creates the
climate and introduction to the house of Muses.
(Photo: Lorenzo Anas.)

hollowed out in its entirety. Before the client contacted Munoz, the original interiors had been destroyed and turned into a completely empty and clear space.

The design process began at the moment of commission. Munoz first researched the history of the building, to establish in a parallel way two dialogues of different nature: one, on the material world with the client, and the other, on the immaterial world with the space. Trying to find what is traditionally known as the *genius loci*—the pervading spirit of the place—she learned that the structure had been the subject of many architectural designs over the years, but that its original interiors had been in the modernist style.

Like in a dream Munoz planned the color schemes reflecting on modernistic interiors dating from the years when the building was built. The 1950s and 1960s had been a time when this building provided shelter for lively meetings between artists and architects. With that in

Preliminary color studies lead to the search for the substance of our ideas. Searching for materials among all the products in the market for the most appropriate things to work with, such as the proper woods and tapestries for chairs and settees. (Photo: Lumen Oviedo.)

Cool colors are located above, with
warmer colors arranged in areas near to
the floor. (Photo: Lorenzo Anas.)

mind, she searched for ideas of color form reminiscent of the period and reflective of the
designs of an early modern style of architecture,
interior design, and color palette.

Because the building had a short-lived but
lively history, Munoz had the sense that some
Muses must be living there . . . and thus discovered the name for the cafe—Musaeum. This
evocative word is one that, proceeding from

Detail showing the neutral colors which predominate over the conversation spot at the rear of the Musaeum Cafe Bar. (Photo: Lorenzo Anas.)

Latin, should mean something like *house of the Muses.* But when you pronounce it, it sounds like *museum.*

As with bygone days, when many museums were erected, Munoz played with the idea of evoking the color atmosphere of a coffee house at Parnassus, that mythical place where artists of antiquity built the symbolic kingdom of poets, and the abode of the nine divinities who preside over the liberal arts, particularly the humanities or poetry. The vision of an empty space, in which all references to history had been destroyed, now began to throb in her mind. She began working with colored pencils and decided to discard all of the literary fantasies coming from Clio, Euterpe, Talia, Melpomene, Terpsichore, Erato, Polimnia, Urania, and Calliope, the Parnassian divinities of history, music, comedy, tragedy, dance, elegy, lyrics, astronomy, and eloquence.

"Working in environmental color design means to solve communication and design problems that have to do with health, signaling, and artistic feeling. Environmental reading changes with geographical, climatological, and cultural conditions—which are the factors that, together with the media and trends, have influence in the development of contemporary social experiences."

Begona Munoz
Principado de Asturias, Spain

During the next phase of the work, mythological dreams disappeared altogether. The creative design consisted of sketching color flecks over the plans. In dirtying papers with color pencils, little by little the flecks took form, and Munoz imagined people entering, staying, and going out . . .

As Munoz continued to visualize the use of the space, chromatic abstraction vanished and the process of design led her to face up to functional, sociological, and operative realities. The initial phase of work with colored pencils now

Translucent hand-painted glass gives a soft light to the staircase leading up to the first floor of the Musaeum Cafe Bar. (Photo: Lorenzo Anas.)

led to a second phase, where color systems, standardized color cards, and computers served as better tools to objectively define the color that each of the composition's elements required.

When the color design was done, Munoz had to visualize the materials and communicate to the different guilds what types of products were necessary for the project. She used, for instance, a color card based on ACC—a color system easily identified by the workers—to describe some of the colors as follows:

The curved surface with its rosy hue, which seems to be reflected on the surreal tops of the tables, gives refuge to the clients. The curve's sweetness is balanced by a broken line drawn by indirect lighting and the cool colors of the terrace that is seen from the room through the large rectangular back window. (Photo: Lorenzo Anas.)

Ground Floor: Ceiling 1. . . . B-034

Ceiling 2. . . . B-174

Ceiling 3. . . . B-192

Ceiling 4. . . . Martele 301 (silver gray), Valentine

First Floor: Ceiling 1. . . . D-156

Ceiling 2. . . . A-154

Ceiling 3. . . . D-096

Ceiling 4. . . . D-042

This description was integrated within a schematic plan that showed the zoning of the ceiling and its color codes. Munoz used similar methods to describe walls, flooring, furniture, lighting, and every other element of the interior design.

Living room. Gentle colors with varying soft muted grayed greens on the walls, trim, and ceiling, create a comfortable room with a relaxed atmosphere. The chestnut red cherry cabinets alongside the oriental rug make up a complementary color palette, for a balanced color environment. (Photo: Doug Salin.)

Dominance, Subordinance, and Complementaries

This beautiful home has a spectacular view of San Francisco Bay. The green trees, and the bay water, which at times turns a lovely gray/green, played pivotal roles in the color selections. The colorist for this project was Lynn Augstein of Sausalito, California, who specializes in color for architectural treatments.

"Color is one of the most influential design tools one can use to express a feeling. As a colorist, it is my job to interpret, translate, then communicate the architect's intent. Color and light enhance and accentuate the beauty of the materials being used. Each color elicits a physical and psychological response; therefore color can amplify an emotional experience, both positively or negatively, depending on how it is used in architecture. The message between color and architecture must be unified in order to work harmoniously both visually and emotionally."

Lynn Augstein
Sausalito, California

The designers were Shawn Hunt and Rick Sambol, the contractor was Bo Potts, the painter was Lance Phillips, and the tile artisan was Mike Schubert. Lynn believed that a cool, soft green would perfectly reflect the environment and enlarge the space, and hoped that her clients would like it as well. (The color turned out to be a favorite of theirs.) Furthermore, the palette, which also consisted of soft rusted reds, peaches, and lush chestnut browns, combined handsomely with the home's blond maple floors and was awesomely complementary to existing furnishings and an impressive art collection, which is a focal point of the environment. The color scheme brought a new vibrancy to the art.

Lynn began the work from an emotional perspective by "feeling" the space. She evaluates the internal and external environment, the amount and nature of the natural and artificial light in the space, its function, and her clients' objectives. The last-noted element is fundamental in all color work. Are the clients active or calm people; are they outgoing or introverted; are they bold or sensitive? Which colors will harmonize with their personality type(s)? Which colors will work to enhance their mood(s)?

Then, moving on to a more practical level, she tours the space with her clients, learning their color preferences and prejudices, and determining which items will remain in the room. Before she ends this first visit, with color sample box in hand she enjoys sharing her initial color ideas, based on the freshness of the experience and information. This early palette is often highly influential regarding, if not the basis for, the ultimate color direction.

Lynn then returns to the studio for a more concentrated and definitive look at the test palette. She chooses more sample colors to allow for what she believes are appropriate options tailored to her clients' needs, desires, and well-being.

Again back to the job site, again with her sample color box. Included this time, however, are the new options for assessment. Lynn knows from experience that some colors may be a good match for the environment but will not resonate with the clients. She is prepared to relegate some colors to the rejection pile. During this meeting, she discusses which wood species will be used in the rooms, and the finishes and stain possibilities.

Color Maps. A description detailing color locations in each room, with color numbers and a small sample of each color, are necessary for the painting contractor. (Photo: Doug Salin.)

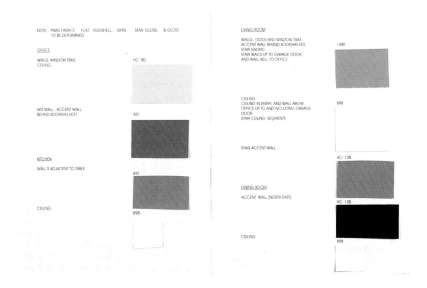

Once the final palette is chosen, the colors are tested in the environment with paint samples on the walls. Paint samples, though they sometimes work directly from the manufacturer's can, most often do not. Typically they need to be modified to get the perfect color. Paint color sampling on the wall should be generous, as a tiny sample will not project an accurate impression. One must be able to look at the prospective color without interference from the existing color. Once the color is set, Lynn asks her clients to live with the sample for a while, because color varies greatly in appearance from daylight to evening light.

Lynn often employs a "common-thread theme," which means carrying some part of the

Paint from a can may need to be altered a small amount. Here are examples of paint brush-outs, with a variation of color pigments added to the original color. (Photo: Doug Salin.)

Dining room. Variations on green give this space visual depth and interest, while defining the areas. The colors selected for the walls work well with the original art. (Photo: Doug Salin.)

palette throughout the home. She uses paint colors and accent pieces, either in the art, furniture, or fabric. The function of a room may warrant an emotional shift from a design perspective; nonetheless this common thread is still possible, is often desirable, and fosters a sense of cohesiveness. Attention is also required to determine

Master bedroom. The warm, rusted, saturated
bisque color that serves as a backdrop for the
visually rich marble accentuates the unique
coloring in the tiles and at the same time reflects
a color which will complement any skin tone.
(Photo: Doug Salin.)

the degrees of color contrasts and balances,
both of which affect human vision. The color
palette we live with has a profound effect on the
way we feel. It can add to or detract from our
interest and comfort without our realizing it—
we often don't know why we feel the way we
do. Color will make the difference between a
room being inviting or foreboding.

Home entertainment center. Creamy butter
yellows, chestnut brown, and again, the soft
grayed green walls in the hallway beyond,
continue the upstairs theme with a common
thread from the main color theme. The warm
tones make this an inviting and very livable space.
(Photo: Doug Salin.)

PART III

Cultural and Public Institutions

Color materials for architecture are increasingly diverse and appropriate to the climate and cultural and economic circumstances of the building type. The architect's needs and design aspirations, together with the wisdom and talent of the professional colorist, meet the demand for an endlessly varying range of formal challenges and solutions.

A typical mosque entrance in the Middle East is richly textured and colored with patterned tile. (Photo: PDR & Partners, Architects.)

Color Context and Integration

In an inspired essay in his book *Color and Context: The Architecture of Perry Dean Rogers and Partners,* Michael J. Crosbie writes that "in a city noted for its architectural conservatism, the work of Perry Dean Rogers & Partners is anything but." The Boston firm's commercial and institutional projects are exciting in their use of bold form and dramatic color, articulate in their expression of materials, and sensitive to their context. A trademark of these architects' work is the use of saturated color to enliven spaces. In many of their projects, color defines the building's constituent parts, and how they work together.

For a new U.S. Embassy complex in Amman, Jordan, where they faced an architectural context far from that of New England, the architects relied on a sensitivity to what is already there, studying methods of construction and the use of ornament native to the Middle East region. Although materials in Jordan are virtually restricted to native stone, the designers derived a richness from this limited palette through the combination and juxtaposition of smooth and articulated surfaces, using ground and rough-cut stone. The context of intense natural light, of surfaces grazed with the desert sun, is much of what inspires their design for the embassy.

Present, too, are stylized interpretations of native ornament in diamond-shaped window grilles and intensely orange doors—geometry and hues common to the products of Bedouin weavers. The embassy complex embodies a seamless integration of context and color, with one reinforcing the other. Buildings are faced primarily with white stone, with orange, yellow,

The entry to the U.S. Embassy complex in Amman, Jordan, features native stone with accents of bright color. (Photo: PDR & Partners, Architects.)

A shop in Jordan, with bolts of fabric
and drygoods indigenous to the region.
(Photo: PDR & Partners, Architects.)

The northeast corner of the U.S.
Embassy in Amman is distinguished by
simple forms and bright colors. (Photo:
PDR & Partners, Architects.)

A gently curving wall of native stone graces the west entry to the American Club in Amman. (Photo: PDR & Partners, Architects.)

"From a limited palette a richness is derived from the combination and juxtaposition of smooth and articulated surfaces, with ground and rough-cut stone. The context of intense natural light, of surfaces grazed by the desert sun, is much of what this design is about. Present, too, are stylized interpretations of native ornament, in the diamond-shaped window grilles and intensely orange doors— geometry and hues common to the products of Bedouin weavers."

Perry, Dean, Rogers Architects
Boston, Massachusetts

green, and black stone used as accent and decoration. Gardens and pergolas, created as special enclosed green spaces, tie together the white stone forms of the buildings.

The interior design also affirms the architectural traditions of the local context. The boldness and massiveness of Middle Eastern building forms with their large masonry units are effectively counterbalanced by the traditional fine detailing of wrought iron grillwork and wonderfully intricate mosaics. The mosaics also enliven the bold architectural forms with an interplay of contrasting light and dark colors.

Reception area in the U.S. Embassy.
(Photo: PDR & Partners, Architects.)

Cubic and cylindrical forms crown
the north facade of the
ambassador's residence. (Photo:
PDR & Partners, Architects.)

Institutional Identity

The office of Sussman/Prejza in Los Angeles, California, plans color for a variety of large to small architectural commissions, entertainment parks, urban revitalization projects, and public and private corporations and institutions. The spirit and exuberance characteristic of their many award-winning national and international commissions (such as the 1984 Los Angeles Olympics, and the 1985–1986 Horton Plaza Restoration project in San Diego) can also be experienced in a very recent project, the Children's Institute in Los Angeles. A synthesis of interior and exterior color space and identity

Aerial view of architectural model for Children's Institute International, Los Angeles. (Photo: Tim Griffith.)

has been carefully and joyously orchestrated to lift the spirits of troubled and homeless children and to provide a glowing environment of hope for the future. The 24,000-square-foot facility is one of the latest collaborative efforts between architects Barton Myers Associates and Sussman/Prejza in a relationship that has had a long and successful history.

As environmental graphic designers and architects, Sussman/Prejza often works through various preliminaries for a given project, generating color studies in the form of drawings, three-dimensional models, and computer-generated images. For the Children's Institute,

Entrance to Children's Institute in model is expressed in warm inviting palette. (Photo: Tim Griffith.)

Actual entrance to Children's Institute,
as realized from color and model
studies. (Photo: Tim Griffith.)

the necessity of planning color in three-dimensional models was important for the realization of a warm and cheerful atmosphere for young children.

Part of the challenge for Sussman/Prejza was to transform the interior into a friendly, home-like environment on a low budget, using paint and color. The facility consists of a child play area, nurseries for abused children, and staff offices. Barton Myers Associates created an interior "urban park" for the play area, which is surrounded by nurseries reminiscent of city row

"To a large extent we are involved with color simply because our work is environmental. Once the work is built, a decision has to be made what color it is [going to be], even if it's white. Yet even this does not fully suggest the importance of color in our work. It is dispersed into everything; it is part of every single project we have ever done. We treat it the way a painter would: We adopt the attitude that we have access to it, and that it is inherently unlimited. This does not mean that we always use it to make bold statements. It can just as easily be subtle or restrained. Not all painters choose to use a lot of colors. Color, after all, can express a full range of ideas and emotions, just as other symbols can. The meaning of an architectural color scheme depends on its surroundings. The term "colorful" is overused, and describes nothing. Can you imagine appraising a piece of exquisite, moving, or complex music as nothing more than "musical"? The use of color is intellectually developed. As with form, it is a metaphor, or a part of a metaphor. As with other aspects of our work, its use is driven by a central idea specific to the project at hand. Color isn't the solution; the solution is expressed through color. In practice—even when an assignment is limited to color—color can't really be isolated from other graphic elements in the built environment: typography, shape, and three-dimensional forms. Color is integral."

*Deborah Sussman
Culver City, California*

houses. Sussman/Prejza gave each nursery a single identifying color. Bright, fresh colors were selected for the facades, creating a joyful atmosphere that seemed appropriate to this child's world. Calming, warmer tones were used in the nursery interiors and staff offices. Also on the inside, analogous hues color the walls and

View of model with theme of nurseries expressed as row houses on various interior facades. (Photo: Tim Griffith.)

Actual color facades of interior row houses theme, as realized from color and model studies. (Photo: Tim Griffith.)

fireplace surroundings. The warmth of the interior spaces is emphasized by the Southern California sun streaming through the skylights and windows.

On the exterior, colors were chosen to distinguish the architectural facades from each other to create the sense of a village with buildings

facing a town square. Areas also dealt with were an infant shelter, therapeutic day care center, and administrative and training facilities for parents, foster families, and interns. The exterior colors are gentle, serene, and warm, creating a homelike, rather than institutional appearance.

Bright, fresh colors selected for each interior facade and architectural element. (Photo: Tim Griffith.)

View of interior color facades, in warm hues and soft tans. (Photo: Tim Griffith.)

View of interior facade in soft yellow.
(Photo: Tim Griffith.)

Exterior facades, distinguished in various
hues of soft yellow and orange. (Photo:
Tim Griffith.)

Pershing Square, Los Angeles. Preliminary color drawing for architectonic forms. (Photo: Lourdes Legorreta and Paul Bardajgy.)

Decoration, Symbol, and Coding

The tradition of vivid color in the architecture of Lourdes Legorreta is an important design element, integral to most office projects. Legorreta is responsive to the natural, intense light and characteristic climate of his native country, Mexico, as well as respectful of the architectural heritage of his predecessor, Luis Barragan, who also employed rich, vibrant hues for primary architectural form. With offices in both Mexico City and Los Angeles, California, Legorreta has evolved a personal and dynamic color language and developed many sophisticated methods in color planning for his highly geometric and inventive works. Solana in Dallas and Pershing

Square in Los Angeles are two examples, originally planned and evolved through color design drawings, which thoroughly integrate color with three-dimensional design. Proceeding through model construction, computer visualization, and final renderings, the office uses three-dimensional models, computer visualization, and renderings to consider the whole atmosphere of the color element in terms of how it enhances the building form and interacts with natural and man-made light, city scale, people, earth, plants, and geographic surroundings.

Pershing Square. Preliminary color drawing for fountain. (Photo: Lourdes Legorreta and Paul Bardajgy.)

San Antonio Main Library

The San Antonio Library, designed by Lourdes Legorreta Architect, is a visual celebration of light, color, shape, and geometry that enlivens the inside as well as the outside of the structure. The city wanted a joyful building, in contrast to the stuffy image of older library facilities. To achieve a well-developed architectural language that integrates the library functions and uses, the new facility blends design and function with an appreciation for two other important elements in the facility—art and technology. The exterior is a visual wonderland of shapes, angles, and openings that create an interplay of light and shadow.

"In the office, working on jobs, we talk about color. Sometimes we get it wrong, so it has to be changed. What goes wrong? Usually it's simply that I don't get the emotional quality I am looking for. As happens with true love, every day I love color more and more. I can't live without color."

Lourdes Legorreta
Col. Lomas Reforua, Mexico

San Antonio Public Library. Presentation drawing to explore overall impact of red statement. (Photo: Lourdes Legorreta and Paul Bardajgy.)

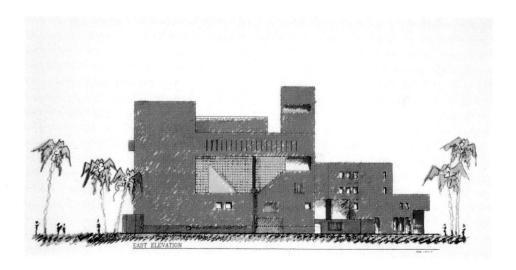

EAST ELEVATION

The color method of the office begins first with preliminary color drawings. In the case of the San Antonio Library, presentation drawings in red were created as studies to explore the idea of an overall red statement without making a final decision.

Then, after constructing three-dimensional study models, the office explored color, applied to the model through trial applications of hue and further sketch studies. An analysis of the site then provided further cues as to the appropriateness of color. The idea of red for the library as a symbol for the city kindled a reaction from the residents, who called it the "Red Enchilada." Other hues used around and inside the building were arrived at by putting samples together on both the model and the building

San Antonio Library. Study model, tested with various hues of red and analogue hues. (Photo: Lourdes Legorreta and Paul Bardajgy.)

San Antonio Library.
Architectural model in context
of site location. (Photo:
Lourdes Legorreta and Paul
Bardajgy.)

Detail of back facade/pool area, with stone walls
in contrast with the red stucco walls. (Photo:
Lourdes Legorreta and Paul Bardajgy.)

Back facade. (Photo: Lourdes Legorreta and Paul Bardajgy.)

during its construction, and determining how the sun reflected light and how the colors related to each other. The large interior lobby was initially supposed to be white. Legorreta, however, decided the interior would be too cold and settled on the final dramatic contrast of a predominately yellow interior, accented with light from the skylights—and the whole atmosphere became warm and inviting.

Central lobby. (Photo: Lourdes
Legorreta and Paul Bardajgy.)

Central lobby (Photo: Lourdes
Legorreta and Paul Bardajgy.)

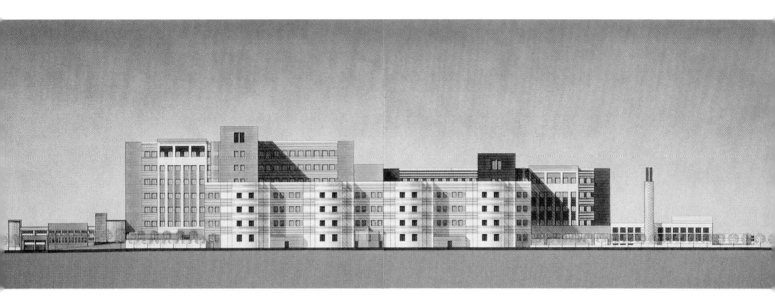

Elevation study, in prismcolor markers and pencils
for Veteran's Administrative Medical Center,
Detroit. (Photo: SHG Incorporated.)

*"Everything in the designer's toolbox must
be brought to bear in the process of
developing large-scale polychromatic
architecture. Typically these tools include:
conceptual sketches, renderings,
computer models, 3-D models, material
samples, large-scale mock-ups, etc.
However, it is very difficult to simulate in
the design process the effects of scale and
distance on the perceptual quality of the
built work. Here, our most reliable tools
are experience and intuition.*

Gerald Reinbold
Detroit, Michigan

Color Function and Legibility

When most people think of a VA Hospital,
images of dark corridors and dim hopes come to
mind. Detroit's Veteran's Administrative Medical
Center Replacement Hospital is designed to dis-
pel this standing stereotype.

With more than 25 years of experience in the
field of architectural design, Gerald A. Reinbold,
vice president of SHG Incorporated, considers
himself an architect who frequently uses color to
enhance legibility, clarify function, and (particularly in healthcare projects such as the Veteran's
Administrative Medical Center Replacement
Hospital and Research Center) promote an attitude of optimism and hope.

Three-dimensional model color study.
(Photo: SHG Incorporated.)

The hospital occupies three full blocks in the mile-long, nine-block Detroit Medical Center superblock. With siting requirements to reinforce the existing setback and green space adjacent to the facility, the program for three major building components included: diagnostic and treatment, medical and surgical nursing, and psychiatric nursing. Each component is expressed as its own building, both in color and massing, and all three are joined by an inner court.

As the project evolved during the conceptual phase, it became clear that a spirit of optimism, clarity of organization, and sense of scale could

Computer-generated four-color "star print"
separation. (Photo: SHG Incorporated.)

be effectively delivered through the use of color.
The question then became one of selecting the
appropriate materials to execute the concept.
The criteria for material selection included:

- Wide variety of colors available
- Permanent, nonfading or chalking
  characteristics
- Reasonably low first cost
- Low maintenance, low life-cycle cost

A local project, the 30-year-old Saarinen-
designed General Motors Tech Center in War-
ren, Michigan, provided inspiration for the
major material: sand-molded ceramic glazed
brick. This material not only met the primary

Built work, clinical block. (Photo: SHG
Incorporated.)

requirements but offered the additional benefits of a subtle range within each color; a tactile, handmade quality; and the desirable images of tradition and solidity. Complementing this material is another material popular in the same era: porcelain-enameled metal panels. Used as cornices, copings, sills, column covers, and spandrels, these panels provide brightly colored

Built work, front entry. (Photo: SHG Incorporated.)

accents with the same assurance of permanence as the glazed brick.

Just as the plan is a three-part composition, the articulation of the hospital's exterior uses a palette consisting of three saturated colors and three neutrals to identify the three major building components and to create a system of pattern to further break down the scale. The primary facade, along John R. Street, is articulated as a tripartite composition in which the two main nursing units are clearly identified and are separated by the silver tones of the third unit, which identifies the main entry. Overlaying this composition is a second layer of smaller tripartite compositions of vertical elements offering a reading of the facade as an urban streetscape. The exterior color concept is also carried through on the interior, providing an additional aid in way-finding, and creating a cheerful and optimistic environment.

Icons, Themes, and Images

John Outram, a British architect known for his provocative use of interior and exterior color and decoration, believes in an architecture of ideas and themes. His use of building materials and his innovative applications of color, texture, form, and space have been considered a new visual language for interior and exterior design and surface treatments. As he believes that buildings and their inhabitants interact in fundamental and subconscious ways, his architecture employs ideas and themes to create thought-provoking spaces. His recent commission for the new Computational Engineering Building at Rice University in Houston, Texas, surrounds a striking and colorful interior with a deep facade of brick and precast concrete. The design successfully bridges across the academic landscape of various departments with the physical attributes of large interior distances between offices and internal functions. The interior vistas catch the eye, as do the building's exterior materials, which harmonize with the campus. But most of all, it is the visual language of Outram's ideas—an extension of material innovation and design research—together with his narrative for the project at hand that create an extraordinary lively and provocative environment.

The primary goal for Rice University's Computational Engineering Building was to forge a new community by bringing together a diverse group of people, all focused on the application of computation to problems of engineering, and somehow inducing them to collaborate.

"Colored and patterned concrete is the material of choice in our practice because it is free to assume any color, form, and pattern. To be set free from constraints in this way is the precondition of modernity. Concrete is solid and heavy like stone, with all the properties of a traditional building material; it even grows lichen like stone. Orange lichen looks good on gray-green concrete, aging in a beautiful way. Beyond this, color is conceptual, adding an idealistic aspect to the gross materiality of a building's fabric. There is no building technology of color, no 'high tech' of color. Color is just pure idea, pure intellectuality, pure emotion. Color animates, bringing the past and the future into the present. Color makes things come [toward] life."

John Outram
London, England

Outram's approach to social organization and his concepts of an occluded temple and river valley civilization, together with an inspirational approach to the building's entablature and surface, all became significant metaphors to accomplish this goal.

Outram believes that the exterior decorations on a building should relate the structure to the various communities and cultures that form its context. One of the fundamental ideas underly-

Entrance facade, Computational Engineering Building, Rice University, Houston, Texas. Although partially obscured by the rich landscape, color and pattern are nevertheless visible and inviting. (Photo: John Outram & Associates, Architects.)

ing this building is the notion of an idealized but obscured temple. For example, the columns in the main entrance bear icons and decorative elements drawn from Mayan, Neoplatonic, Vedic, and Greek mythology and cultures. Also of critical importance to Outram's approach to

Column detail. (Photo: John Outram & Associates, Architects.)

The "Vedic" wing and balcony. (Photo: John Outram & Associates, Architects.)

creating communities is the concept of a river valley civilization. The main entrance includes an iconographic representation in glazed brick of Outram's river valley; above the large arches of the arcade are mountings for medallions commemorating figures of historical significance to the building; and the structure is fronted by a two-story arcade making reference to earlier Rice buildings and an original Beaux Arts plan for the campus. Looking at the original plan for the Rice Campus by Cram Goodhue and Ferguson Architects, one can easily see the valley that

Arcade. (Photo: John Outram &
Associates, Architects.)

Outram envisioned and how the campus buildings articulate the river valley plan. The concept
of a river valley, as an arranging principle in
many architectural settings and periods, is also
evident in the interior coloration cascading
down the main staircase onto the multicolored
floor of inlaid tiles.

The building's interior decoration is constructed largely of inexpensive, manufactured
materials and takes three forms: the shapes and
colors of the structure itself, the patterning of

the terrazzo floor, and the ceiling of the main hall. The structural concrete is exposed in many places. The ceiling is a simple, lay-in, acoustical tile, set at a forty-five-degree angle to the building's grid. The balustrade rails are made from steel pipe. To dress up the interior and imbue these inexpensive materials with a deeper meaning, Outram uses both shape and color. The column yokes, where a round column metamorphasizes into a cage of four square columns, stand out because of their curved surfaces. The color changes in the yoke ensures that the eye "reads" the curves.

All of the surfaces of the interiors are colored from the floor to the ceiling. Outram uses color to convey larger ideas; each choice is rich in symbolism. Color, therefore, is included to convey meaning and to stimulate both conscious and subconscious thought:

- Each floor has a characteristic color matching the scheme of the exterior. Thus, the first floor is blue, for water. The second floor is green, for earth. The third floor is red, for breath. The clearstory is yellow, for fire.
- The long expanse of ceiling is broken by the two halls into eight large rooms. The ceiling in each room has a different color.
- The natural wood doors are stained aubergine, the color of shadow.
- Slab edges, bridges, and the stairs have a blue wave beneath them. This shows that each floor rests on the river's shore.
- The balustrade rail has four colors. The structural members are anthracite and yellow, recalling day and night or time. The green

The entrance hall. The expression of multihued columns, tiled flooring, and painted ceiling create a spectacular fusion of volumetric color. (Photo: John Outram & Associates, Architects.)

The shaped ceiling to the entrance
hall. (Photo: John Outram &
Associates, Architects.)

grid is set in a blue cage, suggesting land surrounded by water or space. Together, they jux-
tapose space against time.

One of the most remarkable aspects of Outram's architecture is the planning and execution
of the ceiling decoration for the main hall. The

Watercolor by Tanya Hunter of the entrance hall.
(Photo: John Outram & Associates, Architects.)

study was created in Outram's office by Tanya Hunter and printed onto canvas by 4-color inkjets driven by computerized information, then transferred to a giant 70- by 50-foot vaulted ceiling. The process, originated by Anthony Chanley of Outram's office, reproduces his A-1 size watercolor painting and explicates its narrative of Cosmic Time.

PART IV

Retailing/Business Applications

Commercial works of color design can be
regarded as problem solving plus inspiration.
The important aspect is that any solution implies
the existence of some problem to which there
have been *other* solutions, and that other solutions to this same problem will likely be developed to follow the one now displayed. The
colorist draws upon the larger context of business principles and practices, marketing, location, competition, and history to assist in both
negotiating successful contractual agreements
and realizing creative production of a high professional level.

Color Design Proposals

The purpose of the proposal is to allow the client to review the full scope of services recommended for a project. Upon client approval and ownership determination, a final contract will include complete terms and conditions and may be delivered in separate and sequential contracts by phase for client signature prior to commencement of work. The following proposal pages from the office of Sussman/Prejza & Company Inc., demonstrate some of the main aspects of a color design service proposal which require discussion and agreement between the color designer and the client.

The title of the project, program description, and purpose of the work are normally first in a sequence of proposal pages which describe various aspects of the work, scope, time frame, remuneration, etc. The scope of the work requires both general and specific information that might take into consideration aspects of color regarding furniture, fabrics, carpet and/or floor covering, paint, laminates, tiles, wall coverings, window coverings, ceiling treatments, special details, and so forth.

Design Analysis and Conceptual Development

Design fees are often based on time involved and the number of persons in the firm doing the work. To develop a general color and material direction for a project, including specific palettes and three-dimensional models, sketches, computer studies, color boards, and

Opposite Page:
Sample pages of a proposal for Design Services from the office of Sussman/Prejza & Company, Inc., demonstrate the title page, purpose, materials program, and planning sequence. (Courtesy of Sussman/Prejza & Company, Inc.)

Page 1

Proposal for Design Services

8 5 2 0
Warner Drive
Culver City
CA 90232
310 836 3939
fax 836 3980

To: CLIENT CONTACT
          CLIENT
          ADDRESS
          CITY, STATE ZIP

Project: Name of Project
          Color Program

Date:

Proposed by: X, Associate
               Sussman/Prejza & Co., Inc.
               3960 Ince Blvd.
               Culver City, CA 90232
               Tel: (310) 836-3939
               Fax: (310) 836-3980

Note:

The purpose of this proposal is to allow the Client to review the full scope of
services recommended for this Project. Upon Client approval and ownership
determination, the final contract version will include complete terms and
conditions and may be delivered in separate and sequential contracts by phase for
Client signature prior to commencement of work.

Page 2

Purpose   Sussman/Prejza & Company, Inc. (S/P) is pleased to submit the
following proposal to _____ (Client) for a new color program for _____
(Project) in CITY, STATE.

The purpose of this proposal is to describe the recommended procedures by
which S/P, working together with Client, will conduct the design study,
documentation, and implementation.

After a description of the scope of work and the NUMBER phases required, this
proposal lists members of the S/P project team with time and cost estimates for
each phase of the Project.

Page 3

Scope of Work   S/P will consult, design, coordinate and assist Client on a comprehensive
                           program to include:

Color Palette &   S/P proposes to develop and select an overall color palette and materials
Materials Program   program for the Client to be used for and applied to the following Project
                           elements:
                           ·   Systems furniture colors and fabrics
                           ·   Modular furniture colors partition inserts
                           ·   Free-standing and loose furniture colors within systems furniture
                           ·   Carpet colors
                           ·   Vinyl floor covering colors
                           ·   Furniture colors
                           ·   Wood base and trim (color only)
                           ·   Restroom tile (color only)
                           ·   Restroom toilet partitions (color only)
                           ·   Counter top plastic laminates (color only)
                           ·   Restroom toilet fixtures (color only)
                           ·   Acoustic ceiling tiles (color only)
                           ·   Door colors
                           ·   Wall colors
                           ·   Wall coverings, where unpainted
                           ·   Window coverings
                           ·   Special details

Page 4

I   Analysis Planning and Concept Design

Color
·   Develop a general color and material direction for Project.
·   Develop specific palettes for each functional area of Project.
·   Develop sketches and/or models to indicate color ideas.
·   Assemble preliminary color and material boards.
·   Develop preliminary ideas for patterns and details.
·   Develop Project criteria.

II   Design Development

Color
·   Finalize all color and material selections by functional area, to include:
    Floor finishes, patterns and colors
    Ceiling treatments and colors
    Paint colors for walls and details
    Wall covering colors and textures
    Office system colors
    Furniture
·   Prepare detailed drawings, models or mock-ups to indicate ideas.
·   Work with suppliers on any special patterns, materials or painting
    techniques, and order samples.
·   Coordinate with suppliers to insure adherence to budgets.
·   Prepare presentation boards.

III   Documentation

Color
·   Prepare color plans and elevations indicating all color and material breaks
·   Specify all materials and colors.
·   Prepare plans indicating all carpet breaks and floor material changes.
·   Assemble costs for all items being coordinated by S/P.
·   Revise presentation.

IV   Fabrication and Installation Administration

Color
·   Review and approve all fabricator samples, mock-ups and brush-outs.
·   Provide on-site observation and coordination for all color elements.

project criteria requires careful consideration. The design development phase may include various aspects of research and material selection including detailed drawings, mock-ups, work with suppliers, and creation of presentation boards. Documentation of the project for execution will necessitate color plans indicating color breaks, specifications of materials, color palette(s), and changes, cost assembly, and revisions to presentation. Finally, the fabrication, installation, and on-site supervision of tests and samples through completed installations, must all be included in the proposal.

In addition, indicating services *not* included is helpful to clarify responsibilities. Discussions of who will be on the project team for each phase and the time frame for each phase are also important. Meetings with clients and third parties should be included in the fees and expenses listed in the proposal. The contract may be broken into phases and itemized as such and totaled. An indication of what are reimbursable expenses is considered along with the fee structure of those in the office who may work on the project. Finally, travel expenses and tax and ownership of the designs and drawings must be addressed.

These ideas, along with descriptions of responsibilities, services, changes, and compliance, are many of the elements to be considered in creating proposals for color design services. Naturally, consultation with legal specialists in design-related professions is always advisable in order to be thorough and confident of the content of your own "Proposal for Design Services"!

Opposite Page:
Sample pages of a proposal for Design Services from the office of Sussman/Prejza & Company, Inc., demonstrate project team, schedule, fees and expenses, travel, tax, and ownership. (Courtesy of Sussman/Prejza & Company, Inc.)

Services Not Included

S/P's services, unless specified under Scope of Work and Procedure, do not include:

- Preparation of special presentational materials, such as detailed renderings, models, fabrication samples or slide presentations.
- Special creative services such as photography, writing, editing, illustration or the preparation of any special artwork such as the generation of additional logotypes and special typefaces, diagrams or charts.
- Implementation services such as printing, fabrication or installation.
- Specialized production services such as typesetting or proofreading.
- Architectural drawings for construction.
- Details for construction or fabrication.
- Design or selection of graphic elements.
- Color or finishes for lighting or furniture.
- Selection or design of lighting elements.
- Design or designation of special effects.
- Furniture selection or design of custom furniture.
- Decorative designs and patterns for or selection of tile, carpet or other materials.
- Research of materials or fabrics for furniture other than those available from the manufacturer.

When required, these services will be provided either by specified sub-contractors and supervised by S/P, or directly by S/P when designated in writing by the Client. Billing for these services will be sent to the Client either directly or as reimbursable expenses.

Project Team

- ????   Principal in Charge
- ????   Associate in Charge
- ????   Project Manager
- ????   Designer

Schedule

The following schedule is a guideline of the minimum time required per phase.

- Phase I   ?? weeks
- Phase II   ?? weeks
- Phase III   ?? weeks
- Phase IV   ?? weeks

Meetings

A maximum of NUMBER meetings with Client and all designated third parties are included in the Fees and Expenses listed below. Any additional meetings held at the request of the Client or necessary to obtain approvals will be charged on a time and materials basis.

Fees and Expenses

Contract Amount

For fees and expenses associated with the services described above, S/P shall be compensated in the amount to follow:

Phase I
Professional Fees	$.
Estimated Expenses	$.
Estimated Tax	$.

Phase II
Professional Fees	$.
Estimated Expenses	$.
Estimated Tax	$.

Phase III
Professional Fees	$.
Estimated Expenses	$.
Estimated Tax	$.

Phase IV
Professional Fees	$.
Estimated Expenses	$.
Estimated Tax	$.

TOTAL:	$.

Note:
Please refer to following section on sales tax and ownership for additional information.

Fees and Expenses

Descriptions

Design Fees

Design fees will be computed on an hourly basis based on the following rate schedule:

- Principal $150.00/hr
- Associate   100.00/hr
- Project Manager   80.00/hr
- Senior Designer   60.00/hr
- Designer/Production   45.00/hr

No change shall be made in S/P's rates prior to one year from contract date.

Total design fees are not to exceed the mutually agreed upon estimate without prior consent of the Client. Billing will be on a monthly basis.

Any additional phases of work or elements, as requested by Client and which are not itemized in this proposal, will require additional time and will be billed in addition to the above outlined estimate.

Reimbursable Expenses

Expenses are estimated based on our past experience. S/P shall be reimbursed for all expenses related to the project. Client will be notified in advance if expenses are expected to exceed the estimated figure.

Reimbursable expenses are in addition to professional fees and shall consist of those expenses incurred by S/P, its employees and its professional consultants in the interests of the Project. All such expenses are to be covered in the Contract Amount listed previously, excluding travel expenses.

Reimbursable expenses are defined below:

- Communication (telephone, telex and telefax), shipping (air and ground), messenger services, packing, postage and freight.
- Reproduction costs to include blueprints, stats, photocopies, laser prints, film and processing, photo prints, acetate color overlays and transfer proofs.
- Materials to include computer disks, art supplies, graphic materials, model materials and photographic materials.
- Special buy-outs to include typography and photo use fees.

All reimbursable expenses shall be billed at cost plus fifteen percent (15%) handling and processing.

Reimbursable expenses shall be billed on a monthly basis and are payable, net, within thirty (30) days from the date of invoice.

Travel Expenses

Travel expenses will include air travel (First Class for principals, Business Class for associates and Coach Class for all others), ground transportation, hotel and living expenses and communication which shall be billed at cost.

Any air travel requested by the Client will be in addition to any above quoted design fee and expenses and shall be billed on a time and materials basis.

There is no air travel anticipated for this project.

Sales Tax & Ownership

Under regulation of the State of California Board of Equalization, should the client wish to retain ownership of designs and drawings, state sales tax will assessed to all fees and expenses incurred on projects located in California as well as out-of-state projects where the majority of its work is delivered within California.

However, if the client does not desire to retain ownership of designs and drawings, only the documentation phase is taxed. Separate and sequential contracts will be issued for Client signature prior to the onset of work for each phase. Without signed separate and sequential contracts, fees and expenses for the entire project is taxed.

All California sales tax is in addition to the above stated fees and expenses and will be added to all in-progress and final billings.

It will be assumed that Client will require full ownership and all fees and expenses will be taxed unless otherwise notified in writing.

Integration and Separation

Gere Kavanaugh/Designs (GK/D), an interna-
tionally known color design firm in Los Angeles,
has been collecting color materials and information for many years, ranging from late-
nineteenth-century paints and color catalogs to
Navajo soil and sand samples collected on
research trips. Many of these items have been
categorized and cataloged on color cards, which
have been made into an office color library. The
depth and range of the library is impressive—as
is the color knowledge of Gere Kavanaugh her-
self. Both are applied to each and every project,
such as the Spectrum Crossroads commission
recently undertaken by her design firm.

Spectrum Crossroads is a 125,000-square-foot
home furnishing center in Irvine, a master-
planned community in Orange County, California. Located on the west side of the I-5 (San
Diego) Freeway at the Lake Forest Avenue off-
ramp, the Crossroads Center is part of the Irvine
Spectrum, a large business, research, and development and industrial complex serving bur-
geoning South Orange County. The developer,
Sanderson-J. Ray Development/GME Equity,
purchased the land from the Irvine Company,
master developer of the Irvine Ranch, which
was originally a Spanish land grant and is now a
major business and residential area.

The Irvine Company only rarely sells
retail/shopping center sites and invariably
retains extraordinarily tight controls on those
properties it does sell, including the right to
approve site planning, architecture, and color
selections. In order to achieve a harmonious

*"Color should be a very important
element for the future: Our [new] cities are
too bland and pretty much the same
throughout the world. This adds to a
depression that need not be—color is one
of the easiest ways to relieve this
situation."*

Gere Kavanaugh
Los Angeles, California

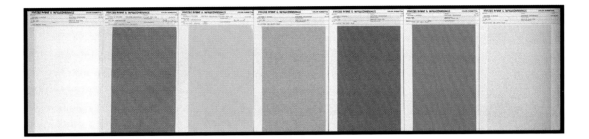

Paint draw-downs for Spectrum Crossroads,
Irvine, California. (Photo: GK/Designs.)

appearance, the Irvine Company chose white at
the outset as the dominant color to be employed
for all buildings in the Irvine Spectrum complex.
Sanderson-J. Ray/GME thus faced the challenge of adhering to the Irvine Company standards while distinguishing the Crossroads retail
project from neighboring nonretail, industrial,
and research and development buildings.

To achieve the desired result, Sanderson-
J. Ray/GME hired Gere Kavanaugh/Designs to
create a color composition that would serve to
simultaneously integrate the center in the overall community and distinguish it from adjacent
businesses. GK/D submitted three sets of color
selections to the Irvine Company for its review
and approval—all of which were rejected—
before finally obtaining approval for a fourth
selection featuring a soft spectrum of light

Efis, an acrylic waterproof paint, applied to a
textured Styrofoam surface to test its color
appearance on exterior building-material-like
surface. (Photo: GK/Designs.)

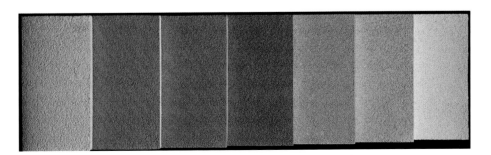

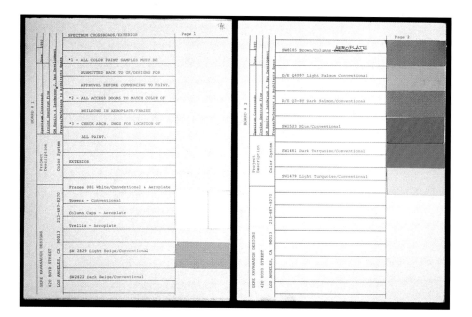

Color boards are created with color chips from paint draw-downs for use by documentation review board and contractor, and for office records. (Photo: GK/Designs.)

beige, light salmon, blue, turquoise, and light turquoise. The tasteful colors and finishes enhanced the design of the buildings, created a very attractive ambience for the center, and satisfied the Irvine Company's insistence on a complementary color scheme. Another important consideration was that the color scheme had to be compatible with major tenants and "pad" users, and blend in with corporate logos and

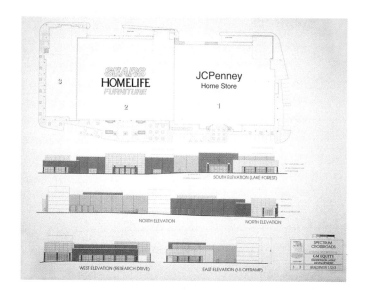

Computer-generated color for elevation views for the Spectrum Crossroads shopping center allows client to visualize color composition and building design together. (Photo: GK/Designs.)

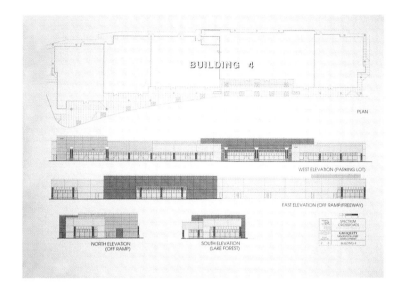

Computer-generated color for elevation views for Building 4, part of the L-shaped Spectrum Crossroads shopping center. (Photo: GK/Designs.)

color palettes. All of the spaces were leased before completion of the center, and in each case the tenant response to color was a significant and positive aspect in the decision to lease.

Spectrum Crossroads is anchored by both Sears Homelife and J.C. Penney Home Store, which is unusual since these two retail giants are natural competitors. Both, however, enjoy success at Spectrum Crossroads, which is 100 percent leased and a commercial success for the balance of the tenants as well as the developer. J. Ray Construction Company was the general contractor and Keisker & Wiggle Architects Inc. of Irvine was the architect of the project. GK/D is now doing the color selections for two new Sanderson-J. Ray/GME projects.

Photo collage of Spectrum Crossroads, with comparative color samples adjacent to each facade. (Photo: Del Zoppo Communications.)

Westbourne Grove Public Lavatories. Male, female, and disabled lavatories with attendant's office and store, and flower kiosk on new pavemented traffic island. (Photo: Chris Gascoigne.)

Generating Attention

In the early 1980s the Royal Borough of Kensington & Chelsea filled in an underground public lavatory at Westbourne Grove in West London and erected a temporary arrangement on top. When ten years later the borough published plans for a permanent replacement and associated landscaping, the Pembridge Association took exception to the mediocrity of the design and commissioned CZWG to propose an alternative for lavatory and landscaping within the council's budget. After many vicissitudes and strong pressure from the association, the council's various committees accepted the alternative, and it was built and completed in July 1993.

By rearranging the inefficient car parking layout, an entirely new triangular island was formed. Variegated trees, cycle stands, and specially designed benches donated by the association are arranged on plain paving with granite curbs.

The new lavatory building stands toward the southwest corner of the island. The turquoise glazed brick walls are parallel to the curb edges to form a triangle. Continuous horizontal louvers line the top of the walls to ventilate the internal spaces. The projecting canopy roof is rectangular, with a fan-shaped end. This geometry allows the central gutter to fall toward the wide end. The internal spaces are daylit through the translucent covering. The sharp end of the triangle is a glazed brick plinth which is partially enclosed with plate glass to form a flower kiosk, an idea added to the brief by the association (as was the large clock on the southwest corner, which was also given by the local residents).

The wider end of the building houses the public lavatories, which can be entered from either side via an open lobby leading to the disabled lavatory and cleaner's room at one side, with the remainder split into male and female facilities by a service corridor under the central gutter. This passage is front-ended by the central attendant's kiosk, which can overlook the lavatory entrances, and has views out. Dancing silhouettes on the steel entrance doors advertise the building's use when the doors are open and celebrate the yearly passing carnival.

Family of Objects

From the beginning of his career, Tomas Taveira's architecture has embraced diversity and color, with a particular concern for the context of Lisbon, Portugal. His rejection of early modern form has led him to explore color, form, and space in a highly personal vocabulary that reaches across boundaries of geometry into the figural expression of the massing of forms and vivid chords of color which resonate in the minds of the Lisbon people. Currently a professor of architecture at the Lisbon School of Architecture, Taveira looks back to his earlier works (which included such subjects as concrete prefabricated housing projects outside of Lisbon) as a reflection of his rejection of "Puritanism" in favor of an environment rich in color, texture, and human scale. More recently, his work in the theater and mass media has included set designs for stage and television productions, lending more diversity and fertilization to his overall approach to human architecture.

Taveira's color design method is closely intertwined with the architectural design process: In fact, they are simultaneous. He thinks and dreams of forms and spaces rich in color texture, scale, and juxtaposition with one another. "Color plays an important role in all of my investigations," states Taveira, "and is not used as a simple technical device. Color is an 'intervention' almost autonomous and the most important linkage with form."

His work is a continuing exploration into the visual complexity and excitement of urban design in contradistinction to either a Funda-

"Color is the secret love of 'design.' Color is the visual art characteristic that enhances creativity, liberty of creation, and radical attitudes in order to create a spectacular and unprecedented art object or environment coming from the imagination and soul."

Tomas Taveira
Lisbon, Portugal

mentalist or a neorationalist aesthetic—whose patterns, used worldwide without profound criticism, provoked a new, boring, and sometimes refined International style.

With projects currently under construction in Lisbon, Taveira's "Objects of Desire" is an extension of a very old movie studio which is today surrounded by a crumbling architectural environment. The building attempts to react to the "site." The twin towers, more "freestyle" than "deconstructed," are to be used by television and cinema producers, and the ground floor

Bird's-eye view of twin towers for television and cinema production facility, in Lisbon, Portugal, rendered in colored pencil. (Photo: Tomas Taveira, Architect.)

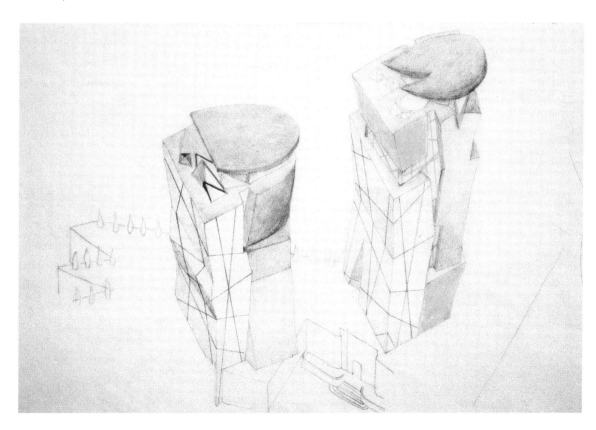

Computer-generated achromatic mass model study of twin tower scheme. (Photo: Tomas Taveira, Architect.)

Computer-generated color composition for twin towers scheme. (Photo: Tomas Taveira, Architect.)

and basement are dedicated to film production labs and studios for shooting advertising and television sitcoms.

Taveira's design method for creating architectural color begins with shapes and forms imbued with vivid hues, in elevation and perspective studies created with color pencil. He also uses computer-generated three-dimensional models (crafted using Corel Draw and Photoshop) which enable him to carefully shape symphonic relationships of color, scale, and architectural detail into harmonic and often surprising cacophonies of visual stimulation. The computer-generated imagery acts as a kind of imaginative chameleon, where he applies numerous sets of various colors. This action of painting and research on possible sets of colors is highly important to the final decision. The final coloration of the building involves the application of ceramic tiles and research conducted with ceramic tile companies in Portugal.

Another Taveira proposal, to be integrated into World Expo '98 in Lisbon, is a multipurpose center to include banking, a hotel, and a shopping mall. This complex involves six aspects of architectural design, each one with a special form and color, unified by a semicircular object behind. This project can be compared to the result of an "explosion" more than a "deconstruction," because of the influences of postmodern vernacular, Russian Suprematism, Deconstruction, and the spirit of the site. This work echoes the new spirit of a "freestyle" of architectural design in opposition to the previsible type of forms that are so closely associated with the rationalist approach. Taveira's

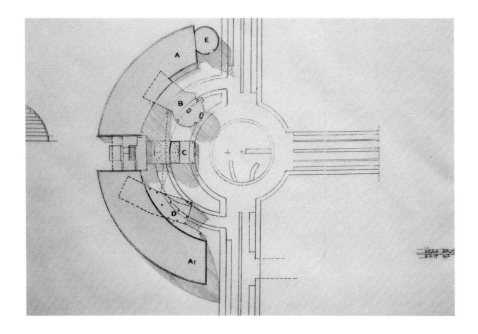

Preliminary design drawing plan study in colored pencil for World Expo '98 Center in Lisbon, Portugal. (Photo: Tomas Taveira, Architect.)

approach is to reinvent an ancient form of architecture and urban experience using color, as in the Mycenaean civilization, where color in architecture symbolized nature and a unification with the visual weight and human scale of architecture.

Preliminary design drawing elevation in colored pencil for World Expo '98 Center. (Photo: Tomas Taveira, Architect.)

Computer-generated model study of the
elevation view for World Expo '98 Center.
(Photo: Tomas Taveira, Architect.)

Computer-generated model study aerial view for
World Expo '98 Center. (Photo: Tomas Taveira,
Architect.)

External night view of Cube Bar, London. (Photo:
Madigan + Donald, Architects.)

Sign and Image

The London architectural firm of Madigan and
Donald approaches design from an intellectual
and scholarly point of view. The richness of
these architects' method and style is reflected in
a recent project, the Cube Bar, which inhabits a
former bank in a multilevel adaptive reuse project in London's Swiss Cottage district, north of
Regent's Park.

"Contemporary science provides contemporary artists, architects, and designers unlimited access to a phenomenal range of polychromatic media with which to express and represent ideas . . . however, colors are not out there in the world—not an automatic correlate of wavelengths—but rather constructed in the branch. . . ."

Stephen Donald
London, England

The Cube Bar is situated at the intersection of the Jubilee and Metropolitan transportation lines and presents itself as an urban oasis for pedestrians anxious for a break from the frantic pace of the city. With signage in cold blue cathode tubing advertising the building as a place for rest and relaxation, highly visible graphics and signage help to frame a dominant window true to the scale and formidable presence of the building towers above it.

The color design was planned in part on a computer to understand the basic composition and possibilities of materials. The interior is a reflection of machine-age materials and a vision of the urban culture inside out. Painted panels and overlapping planes with recessed lighting in deep tones of blue-violet, yellow, and green recall both today's street culture and the Carnaby Street of the era in which the original bank was first opened. The spatial ambiguity between levels of cafe and bar is visually inseparable, allowing one space to flow into the next without artifice of separation. Colored lights recessed into the walls, ceilings, and under the bartop define all of the geometry of color panels and planes into a glowing spatial statement. Colored light is also directional and pulls the visitor into the space, acting as a visual cue to explore and read the interior design as a three-dimensional abstract composition. The Cube Bar is more than a bar. Reflecting an architect's determination to explore everything, no matter how modest, as possibly being beyond the literal reality of its material, it is a celebration of the interacting elements of light, color, form, and space.

Computer-generated preliminary color studies
constructed using a Power Mac 7500/100,
modeled and rendered with Studio Strata Pro.
Left to right, from top: Exterior facade; bar area;
detail above bar; and bar area above. (Photos:
Madigan + Donald, Architects.)

View toward bar lounge/seating area. (Photo: Madigan + Donald, Architects.)

View of second-floor bar. (Photo: Madigan + Donald, Architects.)

Detail of balcony edge. (Photo: Madigan + Donald, Architects.)

"Good selection of colors and materials creates the atmosphere of a place. Color planning in architecture regulates the scale of the buildings and articulates the form and structures of the architecture. The entire milieu of the buildings may be given a new dimension of color, space, lighting, or rhythm . . . thus enriching the real space. The color planner works in the planning group in the same way as a musician plays in an ensemble."

Jorma Hautala
Helsinki, Finland

Aleksin Piha courtyard project, Helsinki, Finland. View looking south toward the large expanse of a seven-story building, in yellow with color run from ocher-violet-pink-orange-pinkish on ground floor. Because of its northern orientation, no sunshine falls on this wall, requiring a warm coloration. (Photo: Jorma Hautala.)

Light and Surface

As one of the leading abstract artists and architectural colorists in Finland, Jorma Hautala achieves harmonies of unusual sensibility in color and light, both in his art and in many of his country's most significant contemporary architectural projects. Working with leading Finnish architect Juhani Pallasmaa, Hautala was given a free hand to create a warm and light-filled space in a downtown Helsinki office building area called Aleksin Piha. The newly formed courtyard area, suitable for pedestrian traffic, is surrounded by four six-story commercial buildings that were recently converted into shops, cafes, and places for rest and relaxation.

Hautala's large graphic colorscape on the walls of the courtyard is a response to nature

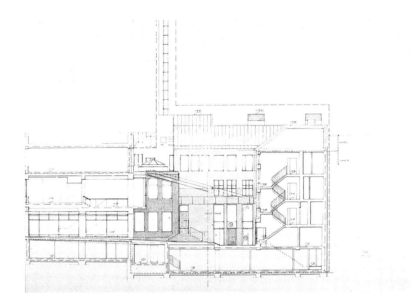

View looking west toward a very small wall, in three warm colors including orange-pink-cream on top. This east-facing wall receives natural sunlight at various times of the year. (Photo: Jorma Hautala.)

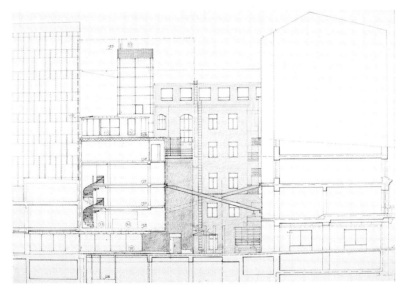

View looking east toward a very narrow wall, in blue with yellow. Sunshine warms this wall in yellow and soft blue-green hues. (Photo: Jorma Hautala.)

and enclosure in bringing the elements of light and color temperature together in subtle nuances of hue and juxtaposition. Each of the four walls was quite distinct in its orientation to the sun, and each received different qualities of daylight. Hautala planned the color using color drawings, with pencil strokes that reflected the

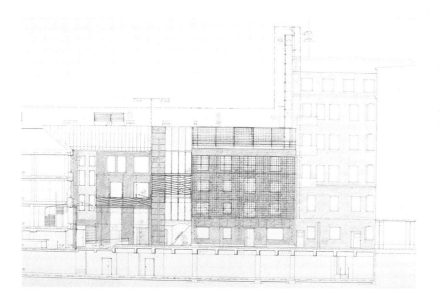

View looking north toward walls in blue, blue-green, and yellow. The cool palette with blue and blue-green contrasts with the steel-grid construction for climbing vines. (Photo: Jorma Hautala.)

Courtyard view facing south. (Photo: Jorma Hautala.)

material sense of the exterior cement treatment through crosshatching and variegated pencil strokes. On the south side of the courtyard looms the large expanse of a seven-story building. No sun shines on this north-facing wall—thereby requiring a warm coloration. Hautala chose yellow, with a color progression from ocher to violet to pink to orange, to also reflect a relationship of human scale to the large facade. On the wall facing west, orange, pink, and cream are used in relation to natural warming sunlight at various times of the year. The sun-warmed wall that faces east is enriched by yellow and soft blue-green hues. The wall facing south received a cool palette of blue, blue-green, and yellow, in sympathetic harmony to the adjacent surfaces and in contrast to the steel grid construction for climbing vines. The courtyard serves as a welcome space for pedestrian relaxation during the summer months, and as a metaphor for light and volume throughout the seasons in this far northern climate.

Aleksin Piha courtyard restaurant and
outdoor cafe. (Photo: Jorma Hautala.)

"Color is the strongest visual tool we use in supporting the presentation of a product. Every color has emotional and physical connotations. Development of these colors and their combinations must be done in a systematic procedure, based on the parameters of the project. Much of the challenge of the project is getting those parameters defined. Once we know what the goal is, color becomes the visual structure supporting the overall effect."

Donald Campbell
New York, New York

Products and Services

Founded more than 15 years ago as a full-service design and display company, Design Etc., Inc. (DEI) of New York City combines a design studio with a visual merchandising department (including lighting and scenic techniques), providing comprehensive design and display services to a wide range of markets.

Over the years Design Etc., Inc. has developed a color system useful for office projects throughout the year. The color palette is made of approximately 120 to 130 colors in 17 color families, and is updated annually. The color system focuses DEI designers once a year on specific color trends and combinations, and during the rest of the year helps them to keep focusing on these combinations.

The development and updating of this palette is directed by Flo Frintzilas, who maintains a careful perspective of color in the design professions throughout the year. The palette from the previous year is discussed, with a review of strong points, weak points, and surprises that developed on projects. Project specification sheets reveal which colors were used most often, and in which scenarios. DEI also reviews color in the toy, home fashion, and gift industries to see how new color trends are developing in products, packaging, logos, and advertising. Once the palette for a product or display is established, additions to it are reviewed on a color-by-color basis. Most often, colors are only added to match logo or packaging PMS colors.

On a specific project, such as the K'NEX Showroom in New York City, the first discussions

K'NEX Showroom, New York City HyperSpace.
(Photo: Barry Pribula.)

First color studies for K'NEX Showroom, included color graphics and three-dimensional color and design campaign. (Photo: Trench Bradey.)

with the client focus on product presentation, product order, room function, and overall mood of the environment. These discussions result in preliminary groundplans and color studies for each of the display rooms. Each individual room must be balanced and focused with color as well as relate to the areas before it and after it. Rough wall elevations are constructed to give a sense of the color story that will be created by going from room to room. DEI's lighting designer, Mike Haristein, is appraised of the color choices and makes suggestions on lighting possibilities (e.g., light gels, flood or pin spot lighting, neon accents, lasers). Key areas in the showroom are locked in first, with surrounding areas adjusted accordingly. Then the secondary accent colors are worked into the overall composition to create a rhythm. Accents in some areas become the focus hues in others. This cre-

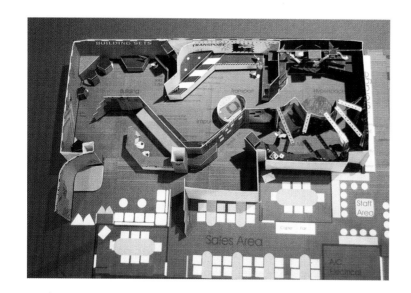

Study model of K'NEX Showroom design. (Photo: Trench Bradey.)

Transport & Trail Showroom area. Color helps to define various sections within the showroom devoted to product segments. (Photo: Barry Pribula.)

ates a tight palette of 12 to 16 colors, which nevertheless is varied enough to create highly different moods.

Once on site, color accents are adjusted, since color studies, models, and test swatches can only go so far in determining how color will work in full scale. After product, packaging, and ad campaigns are placed, the lighting design

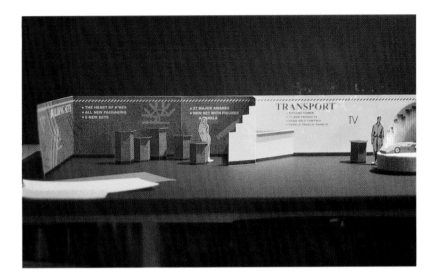

Study model reflects color
definitions between product
rooms. (Photo: Trench Bradey.)

team focuses the lighting to finalize the effect.
Color that appears dull under work light can be
transformed into a rich texture. What is too
bright becomes a softly glowing background.
The overall effect of color is determined by
three factors: the color itself, the surrounding
colors, and the light source. This system might
seem dry and analytical in determining some-

Color used with display background draws the
visitor toward the product, which also carries a
color statement but of smaller and more focused
area and impact. (Photo: Barry Pribula.)

thing that has a very strong emotional response, but determining color choices on a complex display must be based on specific parameters, and not just on colors we like.

In designing colors for a showroom or exhibit, color plans are developed by looking at five criteria points:

1. What is the project and its image?
2. What type of mood is to be achieved?
3. What are the existing spatial and architectural parameters?
4. What are the colors in the surrounding areas?
5. What are the light sources for the area?

This approach to color selection was instituted a little over five years ago, and has helped create stronger displays and environments. With multiple designers working on different aspects of large projects, color balance is difficult to achieve. This system provides a consistent range of colors to work from on any one project, while keeping the flexibility of the full spectrum of color.

Calculated Color Schemes

European designers and architects have provided the design fields with a great deal of visual sensation and excitement in recent years. Partially because of a blend of Postmodern and eclectic tastes, individual solutions to design problems have become prominent, varied, and have enlivened the European design world. The interior design work of Elke Arora of Hannover, Germany, reflects an in-depth understanding of color design marketing and consumer tastes responsive to various ends of the market sectors. Her recent "Bath Boutique" project demonstrates many of the planning factors of color, form, and image that contribute to a successful commercial environment.

Colors are related in context with materials in the design process for the Arora Bath Boutique. The materials themselves have to fulfill the demands, to support a bathroom image. But the atmosphere of "bath" cannot be achieved by the product alone. The overall ambience of the boutique must be coordinated, unified, and coherent.

For this, an atmosphere must be created, through calculated color schemes, that will invite and court the customer. To stimulate the customer's emotions, an integrated whole is necessary, involving light, color, shape, and material. For this target, the following aspects must be coordinated:

- The designer-collection
- The architecture
- The interior-decor

"I believe that anyone who brings color creations to the public has an important responsibility and should have knowledge of the color-psychological functions. Color design must include consideration of the user as well as the nature of materials in the manipulation of form and space."

Elke Arora
Hannover, Germany

This building is but one example of the diversity of existing architecture for shops and stores. Anything in terms of an architectural context of design—such as high-tech, Classicism, Neoclassicism, and Modern and Postmodern styles—is possible in our highly eclectic environment. (Photo: Elke Arora.)

- The product-range
- The customer-target-group
- The label
- The location, the region
- The room
- The colorways, the material
- The level of taste

The architecture is an existing fact in varying completions, at varying locations, in varying regions. The "Arora Bath Boutique" is to be looked at like one little stone of many in a mosaic. The result, for example, would be a shop within a shopping mall or a department store, as opposed to a detached shop. In a newly designed shopping mall, the architecture would become a supporting component of an integrated whole. The interior furnishing is dependent on many factors. The existing room sets the basic parameters: the ground floor plan, materials, lighting, and infrastructure of the building. The interior design is also dependent on the product palette to be presented, and of course on the customer target group.

For interior furnishings, the designer of the interior space and the developer of a color-palette has to bear in mind the legitimacy of color. The customer target group is only

Color samples of bathroom rug yarn. This selection of a few of the hundreds of available colored yarns gives only a glimpse of the multicolored possibilities. (Photo: Elke Arora.)

addressed as a generic term for the description of a group of individuals, and is therefore never a precise, exact measurable concept. One considers various parameters including income, residential area, standard of living, and more. The level of taste is also defined only vaguely, as taste is a constantly changing sensation and emotion.

In response to the given architectural parameters, the use of color for the designing of interiors has limitations and expectations. In addition, the color of the Arora label—purple—is set and an invariable fixed point in the total project. Light, color, shape, and material form a

Interior perspective with three original bathroom rugs. The intention of the unusual style of the presentation—hanging the rugs like banners from the ceiling—is to suggest a new attitude about their function and color design. (Photo: Elke Arora.)

Sketches and collage of sales tables, roller blinds, light fixtures, original rugs, and bathtub. The salesroom can either demonstrate the product elements by concrete examples of their use or by creating an abstract shopping world. (Photo: Elke Arora.)

unit and a visual climate. This climate is carefully modulated through light. The objects in the room and the light which plays on and around them orchestrate a tactile experience. Natural and artificial light are aids to make colors and shapes visible, and to create emotions. The idea is to make associations of color and material easily recognizable. With the attempt to create harmony between the visual elements of the interior designer, the idea and its appearance are the most important goal, to visualize the whole as unity.

Color is event and experience. The material consumption for a good color design is not more expensive than one for a bad color design. Color creates various moods—but these moods can never be precisely defined. Color recognizes no boundaries, but color shades are interpreted in perception easily, and this knowledge is significant for the selection of the color modulation and planning for the boutique.

Collage of original materials for the shop interior. This demonstration of just several of the materials gives an idea of the multitude of product combinations in the interior. Marble, glass, ceramics, stainless steel, chrome, zinc, laminates, plastics, synthetics, paint, and textiles are the components for the harmonious, attractive, and useful interior atmosphere. (Photo: Elke Arora.)

PART V

Industrial Colorations

Ever since Faber Birren identified the positive role of color in the industrial environment during the Second World War, colorists have contributed to transforming the workplace into a safer, more legible, and harmonious environment. The challenge of identifying areas within industrial facilities in need of visual clarification brings the colorist together with management, technical staff, personnel, and architect to find solutions of identity, codification, legibility, harmony, and image.

Aerial view of the Dead Sea Works (Israel) Magnesium Plant in the last stages of construction. (Photo: Judith Ruttenberg, Architect.)

The basic color layout scheme for the plant is as follows:

a) All buildings in which stages of the magnesium manufacturing process are performed have a yellow background color for the walls and roof (active, outstanding color), with graphic elements overlaid in green, white, blue, orange, and pink.

b) All buildings in which service-oriented functions are performed (ready product storage, for example) have a light blue background color for the walls (cold, passive color), with graphic elements overlaid in yellow, orange, white, green, and pink.

c) All electricity buildings have an orange background color for the walls (warm, active color), with graphic elements overlaid in yellow, dark green, white, and dark orange.

d) The main office building has a metallic silver finish for a high-tech, sophisticated look.

e) All pipe racks are green, providing an effect of vegetation contouring the buildings.

f) All elements of technical equipment are painted according to their function. For example, all tanks, silos, and thickeners containing carnallite are turquoise; all conveyors are dark orange; and so forth.

Desert Light and Industrial Color

The magnesium plant built by the Dead Sea Works, Ltd. is the largest manufacturing project undertaken in the Sodom area of Israel. The site on the shore of the Dead Sea extends along the main road to Eilat for a distance of almost a kilometer and is 300 meters in depth from the main road. The main buildings in the project are very large, the most dominant being the two electrolysis buildings, which are each 252 meters long and 60 meters wide. Because of the scale of the project, the management of the Dead Sea Works considered it both a necessity and a unique opportunity to set new standards for an industrial environment—particularly one located in one of the most visually and historically significant areas of Israel.

Judith Ruttenberg, architect and colorist, developed the far-reaching plan for coloring all of

Preliminary color scheme for final product storage. The light blue background is typical to all service-oriented functions. Graphics in yellow, orange, and white emphasize gates and doors, creating the right proportion between their dimensions and those of the elevations. (Photo: Judith Ruttenberg, Architect.)

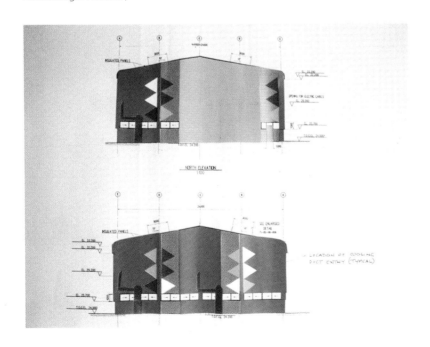

"Because of the enormous amount of visual impact surrounding us, and in order to be able to affect the viewers/users both mentally and psychologically, I believe that I, as a color-designer, must define a very clear and exact color concept. This concept will provide a basic frame on which the detailed color planning will be built. In such way the identity and character of the color planning remains distinct, although the color concept appears in sophisticated variations according to the needs of the specific project. The outcome is always what I call "H.I.C."—High-Impact Color—a color design which has a powerful presence and which makes a strong emotional, mental, and physiological statement in the environment."

Judith Ruttenberg
Ramat-Gan, Israel

the buildings and industrial facilities. The aim of the color design, as described by the management, was "to create a vibrant and exciting project that at the same time respects the awe-inspiring vistas of the Dead Sea area." The magnesium plant is an epoch-making project, bringing an entirely new industry to Israel, and will make that nation one of the few in the world with a magnesium production capability. The project is too important and too big to "hide," and for this reason a bold approach was adopted. Extensive use of vibrant color, both on the outside and the inside of the buildings, and on the huge industrial structures that stand along the side of the buildings, is part of the effort to provide a distinctive character to the project, and to assist in orienting visitors and workers. A color range of light blue, yellow, and orange provides the main colors, with accents provided by green, white, turquoise, and pink. Because these are

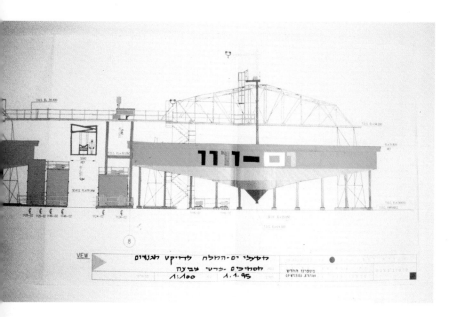

Preliminary color scheme for thickeners. The same color code as for the carnallite silos is used here. Although the two types of tanks differ in size and form, the color design makes it obvious that the same material is being processed. The consistent use of the graphical language creates unity and order. (Photo: Judith Ruttenberg, Architect.)

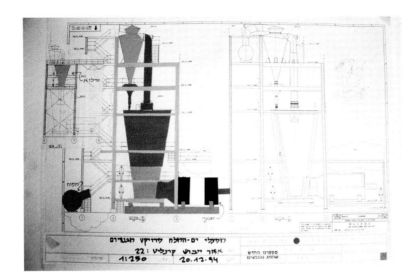

Preliminary color scheme for carnallite driers. Warm colors for the driers indicate their function, while the contrasting turquoise carnallite silo stands out despite being relatively small. The simple graphics enable viewers to perceive the design clearly in spite of the complicated construction surrounding the driers. (Photo: Judith Ruttenberg, Architect.)

colors that naturally occur in the environment, they both establish the extent of the project and complement the natural color tone of the area.

By using unusual and bright colors, working conditions are enhanced and a totally new environment is created—a bold breakout from the stereotyped gray colors often associated with heavy industry. The use of the same colors for the piping, the smokestacks, the silos, and the tanks coordinates the building and external processing elements and at the same time creates a

Examples of color designs for silos. By developing the surface of the silo into modular color rings, an effect of unity is achieved despite the different forms, sizes, and colors of the silos. (Photo: Judith Ruttenberg, Architect.)

Examples of color combinations appearing on the stacks (orange), walls of electrolysis buildings (yellow), and huge pipes (yellow, strong pink). The color scheme reflects a new concept of the right atmosphere for the industrial environment. (Photo: Judith Ruttenberg, Architect.)

stimulating environment for workers and visitors. The color code for the different functions can be discerned clearly: yellow for the different stages of the magnesium manufacturing process; light blue for service-oriented functions; orange for electricity centers; and green pipe racks running along the building providing a vegetation-like frame. To make these colors stand out through contrast, the color of the main office building is a neutral metallic silver (the color of magnesium metal), which also provides a high-tech look. The colorful environment—tanks, silos, equipment, and buildings—creates a dynamic atmosphere and unique industrial site, standing out from the faded background colors of the desert sands, and complementing the blue of the Dead Sea.

Examples of color combinations and graphic design elements for buildings and for the related complexes of steel pipe racks, bridges, stairs, handrails, elevators, platforms, and columns. Notice the effect created: These structures provide a colorful steel background and connecting network for buildings, machinery, containers, and silos. (Photo: Judith Ruttenberg, Architect.)

Harmonies of Color
and Natural Material

We have reached a time when great attention is given to surfaces as well as to shape. In the design process, the three elements in surface treatments—material, graphics, and coloring—represent a vast amount of sensory possibilities, requiring superior technical knowledge and artistic talent to reach the final moment where sensibility and quality come under the spotlight. For Jean-Philippe Lenclos and Atelier 3d Couleur in Paris, the result has been worldwide recognition for the depth of planning, research, and sensitivity with which they bring solutions to life. Our environment holds many opportunities for reconstituting cold industrial forms of factories and machinery into fresh new solutions for a bright and harmonious environment.

La Ciotat is a port located about 30 kilometers from Marseilles, on the shore of the Mediterranean Sea. This city has a remarkable historic character because of the quality of its architecture in cut stone dating from the eighteenth and nineteenth centuries. It is therefore a protected site, not only because of its historic value but also because of the tourist value of this part of the Mediterranean coast, which is so close to the well-known and celebrated Côte d'Azur on the Riviera.

Across from the old city, on the other side of a huge dock, is an important naval shipyard which was expanded between 1975 and 1980. To avoid turning the site into a bleak industrial landscape that would inhibit tourism and summer visitors, a decision was made to conduct

*The French port city of La Ciotat, near Marseilles
on the Mediterranean, with historic buildings
from the eighteenth and nineteenth centuries.
(Photo: Jean-Philippe Lenclos.)*

an impact study of the shipyard as relating
to urbanism, architecture, and color. The
3-Dimensional Color Studio was put in charge
of the color study. The conclusion was to keep
the style of the shipyard's buildings and
machinery within the range of colors of lime-
stone found in the old city. In the space of a few
years the site presented a coherent and harmonious color composition with the color serving
as a common denominator between the industrial structures and the historic city.

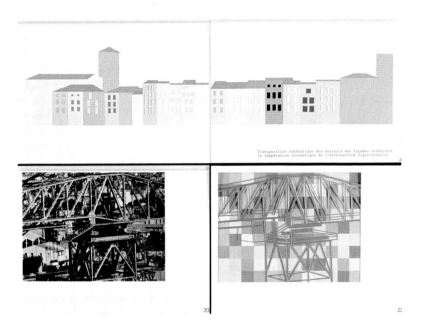

Elevation sketch of colors of characteristic architecture along the coast, with a detail of an aluminum-colored shipyard crane against the historic stone and terra-cotta buildings of La Ciotat. (Photo: Jean-Philippe Lenclos.)

Abstraction of transposition of color pattern samples and of natural materials. (Photo: Jean-Philippe Lenclos.)

A preliminary attempt by the
3-Dimensional Studio to create
a reduction of colors. (Photo:
Jean-Philippe Lenclos.)

Final version: The stone-colored tones of
cranes and machines in the shipyard reflect
the colors and character of the adjacent old
city. (Photo: Jean-Philippe Lenclos.)

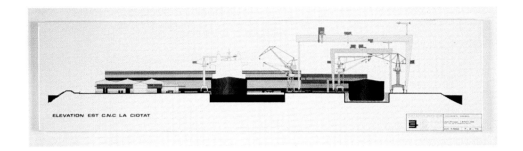

Elevation of several buildings in the shipyard,
showing their final beige, stone, and sand tones.
(Photo: Jean-Philippe Lenclos.)

Completion of shipyard color project, with final
selection of colors. (Photo: Jean-Philippe Lenclos.)

Color Coding and Identity

Another industrial project of Atelier 3d Couleur which focuses on identification of functions in a large manufacturing facility is the Solmer Steelworks. The facility is made up of a vast industrial group built in the mid-1970s, on the Mediterranean coast of Fos sur Mer in the Camargue region of France, not far from Marseilles. The Solmer Steelworks includes a dozen adjunct factories that surround the main production facility: a rolling mill that turns molten steel into steel sheets. The construction project required the involvement of a group of urban multidisciplinary conceptualists, a grouping of

General mass design for the Solmer Steelworks near Marseilles, France. In order to give each area (e.g., primary materials, stock, production, administration) an identity, a color was assigned to each one. In total there were 12 dominant colors. These colors served as references for visual communication. (Photo: Jean-Philippe Lenclos.)

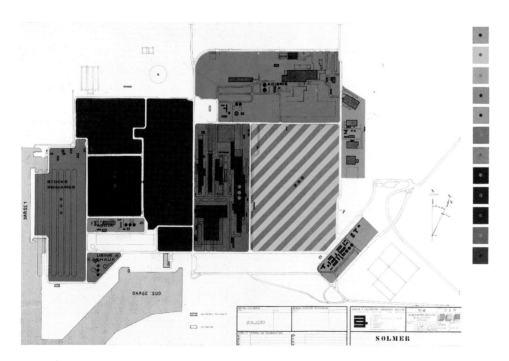

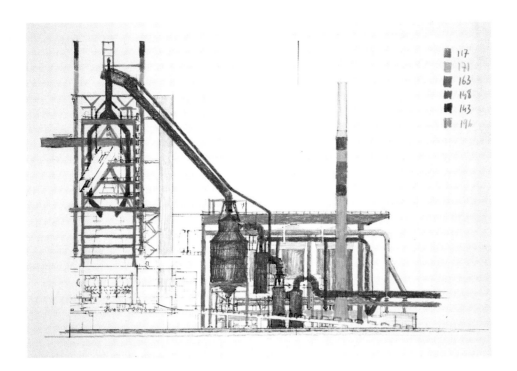

Detailed color pencil sketches were created to work out the color strategy. Six colors were used in the design of the blast furnace. (Photo: Jean-Philippe Lenclos.)

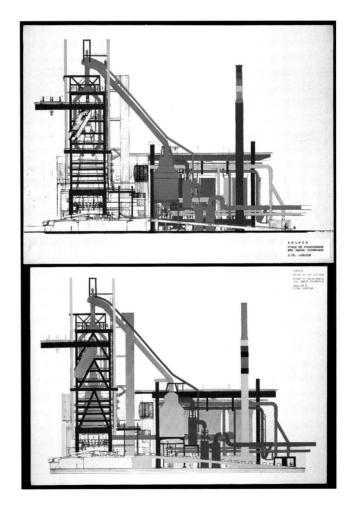

When the sketches were completed they were transposed to a collage model. (Photo: Jean-Philippe Lenclos.)

Primary blast furnace after paint was applied.
(Photo: Jean-Philippe Lenclos.)

urban planners and architects from Studio 9 of Marseilles, a landscape painter, a signaletician, and a colorist—Jean-Philippe Lenclos—for the colored urban plan. The most important buildings in the steel factory are the blast furnaces and rolling mill, which are 900 meters long. The goal was to provide an overall color identity to the various factory and production facilities with 12 dominant colors, and simultaneously provide each building with a color identity within the whole environment.

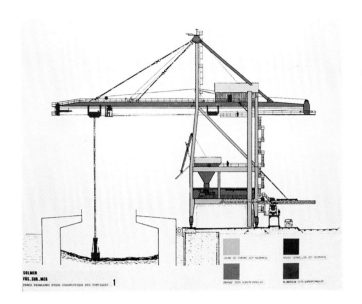

Sketch of colored crane. Four colors from the same range were used on all of the cranes. (Photo: Jean-Philippe Lenclos.)

Two door cranes after being painted. (Photo: Jean-Philippe Lenclos.)

PART VI

Color Formalism in Urban Design

Color has significance to every place. In determining which aspects are significant about an area or region (and which ones may be discarded), it is necessary not only to understand the environment and the immediate demands of the problem at hand, but also to delve into the history and culture of the region to determine whether the attributes of the past are relevant to informing the present and planning for the future.

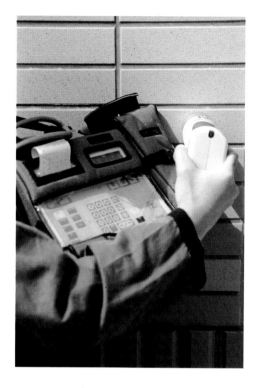

Establishing a color standard for the Faret Tachikawa urban redevelopment project, Tokyo: Environmental color survey of the surroundings by using photoelectric colorimeter. (Photo: Shingo Yoshida, Color Planning Center.)

"Beauty or ugliness do not exist in the color itself. The main issue is how color is used. By surveying the creative colors of the district, the colorist extracts the colors that the district seeks [and] combines it with the suitable shape and materials to deliver a creative and beautiful environment."

Shingo Yoshida
Tokyo, Japan

Environmental Urban Color Planning

Shingo Yoshida studied design at Musashino Art University in Japan and also served as a research fellow investigating environmental color planning for Professor Jean-Philippe Lenclos in Paris. Currently, he is a colorist with the Color Planning Center in Tokyo and instructor of art and design at Tokai University. He has undertaken numerous environmental color projects for urban projects throughout Japan and has received international recognition, including the Stuttgart International Color Design Award, Stuttgart, Germany.

Yoshida's work for Faret Tachikawa, an urban redevelopment project in Tachikawa-shi, Tokyo, was completed in autumn 1994. The formation of a color standard was sought to create a desirable scenery for the redevelopment project. As part of this process, Yoshida surveyed the exterior colors of the surrounding architecture to acquire a feel for color distribution.

Taking into account this relationship with the existing surrounding area, suggestions were made on the base external colors for the planned redevelopment site. Several were then evaluated, and one—to apply a sedate, natural color tone made from the harmonized blend of

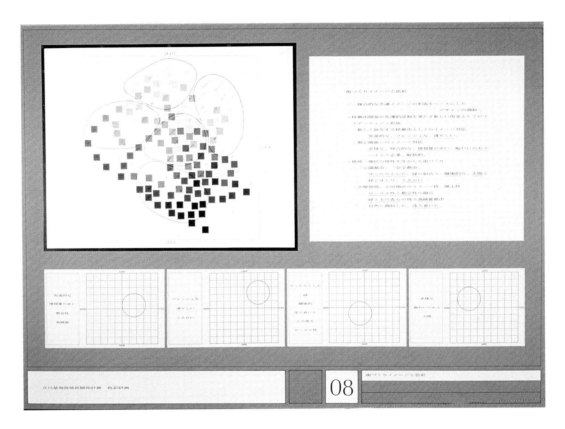

Investigation of color image. (Photo: Shingo Yoshida, Color Planning Center.)

low-chroma color tones—was chosen. For each section of the architecture, the color utilization range was shown by using a Munsell Diagram. This color standard was distributed to the architects, who were required to conform to the color utilization range. Furthermore, by using this standard, external materials of the buildings in the Faret area were documented for color-comparison purposes. At the practical designing stage of the architecture, these materials were lined up on site for comparison with the adjacent architecture, so that adjustments could be made to the color interrelation. By forming a

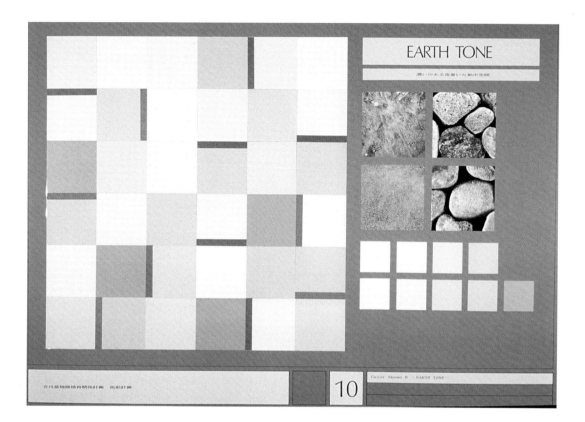

One of several color image proposals. (Photo:
Shingo Yoshida, Color Planning Center.)

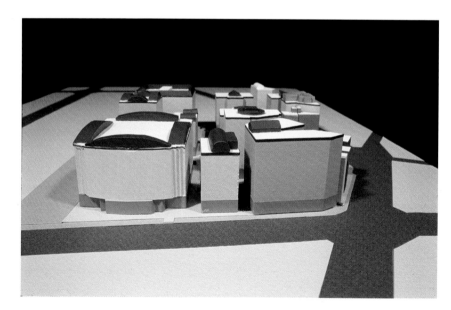

Color investigation by using
model. (Photo: Shingo Yoshida,
Color Planning Center.)

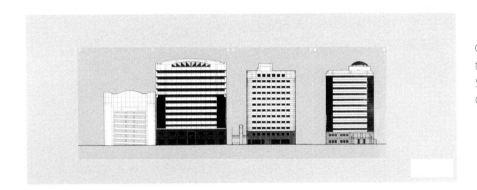

Color investigation by using three-dimensional plan. (Photo: Shingo Yoshida, Color Planning Center.)

Color adjustment by using real external materials.
(Photo: Shingo Yoshida, Color Planning Center.)

An aspect of the completed Faret Tachikawa urban redevelopment project. (Photo: Shingo Yoshida, Color Planning Center.)

color standard and implementing on-site color adjustment, the planners were able to create a community marked by unity and appropriate variation. Since the Faret Tachikawa project, many other major projects in Tokyo have begun to utilize environmental urban color plans to ensure visual harmony between the architecture of the projects and that of the areas surrounding them.

Aerial view of Thames River near London,
England, and the Wimpey Hobbs Ltd., plant at
Granite Wharf in a new context of color and site.
(Photo: Michael Lancaster.)

*"If we think of buildings as conceived and
designed from within, their form and
detail echoing their function, color design
is the opposite, working from outside over
the buildings and their context."*

> *Michael Lancaster*
> *London, England*

Wimpey Hobbs

Opportunities for creating or positively influenc-
ing large-scale landscapes are rare; even rarer
are opportunities for using color on a grand
scale. Yet that is exactly what Michael Lancaster
has begun to do as he plans a color strategy for
the Thames River as it flows along the countryside and through London, England. Lancaster is
a talented environmental color planner, architect, landscape architect, and the author of an
invaluable text, *Colourscape*, which clarifies the

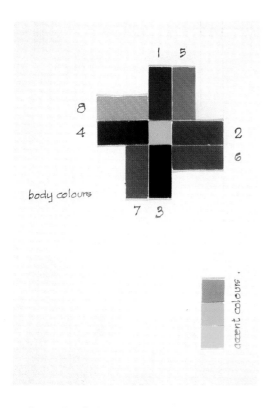

body colours

accent colours .

Four pairs of color combinations which would
harmonize with yellow—the corporate color of
Wimpey Hobbs, Ltd. (Photo: Michael Lancaster.)

place and meaning of color in our surroundings
and provides a solid base for an understanding
of color in the context of the environment.

The color scheme for various nodes along the
path of the Thames being planned by Lancaster—such as the color palette for the Wimpey
Hobbs, Ltd., plant at Granite Wharf, approved
by the London Borough of Greenwich—reveals
both the importance of color and the need for a
coordinated color policy for the Thames riverside. The clients were offered a range of 17
main colors and 10 accent colors for the Colorcoat cladding for their facility. After consideration these were reduced to four pairs of
combinations that would work with the yellow

Color combinations with yellow were
tested in collage compositions and
modified to achieve optimum harmony.
(Photo: Michael Lancaster.)

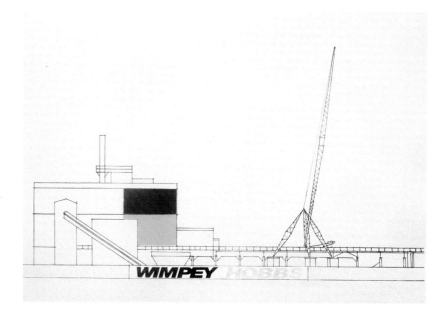

Prior to color application, drab gray-blue factory facades and equipment recede into the light blue sky without distinction, organization, or interest to their forms. (Photo: Michael Lancaster.)

In contrast to the photo above, the application of a basic palette of blue and yellow both grounds the forms and distinguishes aspects of their form and function. (Photo: Michael Lancaster.)

house color of the company. From these studies, the modified blue was accepted as being the most appropriate for the static buildings to relate to the river and the site, with bright yellow for the working parts of cranes and conveyors. These provide a strong focal point contrasted with the blue, which appears to recede into the background.

Introduction

The project of planning color along the Thames includes establishing guidelines for the use of color, both in terms of natural and manufactured materials and applied paints, in order to create a coordinated color composition and to avoid accidental and disturbing uses of color. The project was not intended to impose ideas of "good taste" upon the occupants and developers; on the contrary, certain freedom of choice was encouraged in order to demonstrate the importance of color and its relationship in making an acceptable and exciting environment.

Scope

The scope of Lancaster's study along the Thames was concerned with the riverfront. Proposals relating to building colors were schematic and based upon actual colors (Colorcoat and BSS Paint Industry), while final proposals were related to actual drawings of riverside elevations at an appropriate scale.

Method.   After considering the field of view in terms of object and background, a basic back-

The palette of Colorcoat 2000 high-performance cladding material with accent hues. (Photo: Michael Lancaster.)

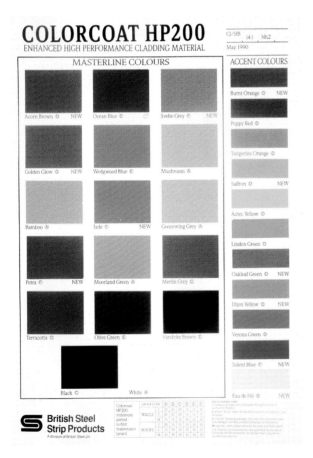

ground palette was established, against which the "foreground" colors could be judged. The background largely comprised the landscape colors of grass, trees, and other vegetation, and the colors of building materials—largely brick in variations of red and yellow, with tile and slate roofs, and concrete. The "foreground" colors are those which stand out against the background. These are frequently areas of white, such as white buildings seen against the dark landscape background rather than against the sky. Along the riverside the predominant foreground colors are those of the larger industrial complexes. The facilities are already exciting on account of their large scale and interesting forms; and color is an added bonus. So far, the latter has tended to be considered in isolation. The intention of this study is to investigate and propose ways in which the colors of the different plants can be coordinated, both with one another and with the background against which they are seen.

Analysis of the Wimpey Hobbs Project

The Colorcoat HP 200 cladding colors provided a useful basis for establishing a rudimentary palette that would be sympathetic. The starting point was "Saffron" in the Accent color range, which approximated the house color of Wimpey Hobbs. With this as a basis, 7 of the 15 Master-line (cladding) colors were eliminated on the grounds of ambiguity, similarity of hue, or similarity of value, leaving 8, together with black and white. Of these, 4 were considered most suitable for use with the Saffron color, on account of their strong value contrast. They included Ocean Blue, Terra Cotta, Olive Green, and Vandyke Brown. The other 4, Wedgewood Blue, Petra, Moorland Green, and Merlin Grey, were considered as possible alternatives, while black and white were deemed unsuitable. Aspects of color contextualism in adjacent buildings were also analyzed and several more combinations eliminated. Preliminary proposals incorporated the house color of Saffron with other combinations of Olive Green or Moorland Green, while subtle variations of this could be introduced by the juxtaposition of Tangerine Orange and Aztec Yellow related to the height of the building; and at the same time, accommodating actual variations in house colors.

Ground-level view of Wimpey Hobbs, Ltd., upon completion of color design. (Photo: Michael Lancaster.)

The Turin Color Plan and the Turin School of Urban Restoration

The far-reaching color research and urban restoration projects of Giovanni Brino, professor of architecture at the Polytechnical University of Turin, Italy, have taken place in a number of cities across Europe. This work has included the establishment and coordination of a unique education program in color restoration (coordinated with SCI-ARCH—the Southern California Institute of Architecture—in the United States), which features on-site experiences in mural restoration, paint formulation, plaster molding, stone work, leaded glass windows, painted and illuminated signage, and urban furnishings.

When Professor Brino was a student in Italy in the 1950s, there were neither specific courses for nor public or governmental recognition of the problem of color and urban furnishings. Subsequently, during one of his earliest restoration projects, on the house of Alessandro Antonelli (the greatest Italian architect of the early 1800s), Brino discovered the home's original coloration plans, prepared in the same year as those for the Crystal Palace, and utilizing a similar hue scheme for emphasizing shape through color. The reintroduction of this original polychromy destroyed a century-old myth about color in Turin, which previously had been viewed as a monochrome patina (Turin Yellow) that had grown in popularity and geographical dominance throughout the city during a century of use.

Up to the late 1970s, some 2,000 facades in Turin were repainted every year, and half this number abusively. At the time the only criterion

"The EEC professional training course aimed at the restoration of facades represents the culmination of a long experiment in the field of professional training, with analysis in the Scuoladi Restauro Urbano in Turin, and the intention of forming technical experts capable of correctly restoring the facades of old towns using traditional construction materials and methods."

Giovanni Brino
Turin Italy

adopted by the Municipality for restoring the facades' colors was the systematic use of the mythical "Turin Yellow." This massive environmental tampering had been going on for decades, often without any control whatever, leading to the gradual destruction of the original city colors which had been one of its distinguishing features (remarked at the end of the nineteenth and early twentieth century by such attentive visitors as Friedrich Nietzsche and Henry James).

The practical demonstration that the so-called "Turin Yellow" was merely commonplace was proven at the end of the 1960s by Giovanni Brino and Franco Rosso of the Turin Polytechnic with the Antonelli facade restoration, based on accurate archive research. On the basis of further systematic research into the archives on the colors of all Turin buildings, the discovery was made of an existing color plan of Turin, drawn up for the entire city, developed between 1800 and 1850 by the "Consiglio degli Edili" (Council of Builders), the body responsible for the urban management of Turin.

In this color plan, the colors of the main streets and squares of the city, characterized by uniform architecture (cf. the attached "Color Map") were planned in a very sophisticated way. In fact the "chromatic paths" leading to Piazza Castello, the city's ideal center, were interconnected by a complex network of streets and squares that were colored in such a way as to form a continuous and at the same time varied sequence of about eight different colors (cf. the attached "Color Palette").

After 1845, in order to further rationalize the color plan procedures, the Council of Builders

The color map and the color palette of the Turin city center, as based on the archive documents. (Photo: Giovanni Brino.)

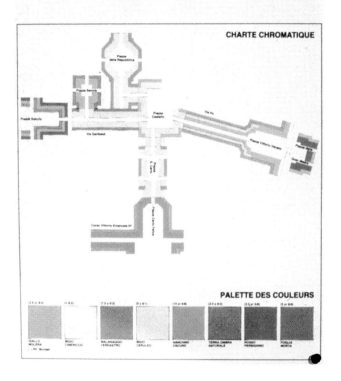

made public the city's "Color Palette," developed in the course of nearly half a century, by having all the most recurrent city colors (about 20) painted on a "sample wall" in the courtyard of the Municipal Building. These colors were marked with code numbers and became the point of reference for the house owners as well as for the house painters and the planners of the Council of Builders. From then on, colors were directly designated in official documents by their corresponding code numbers.

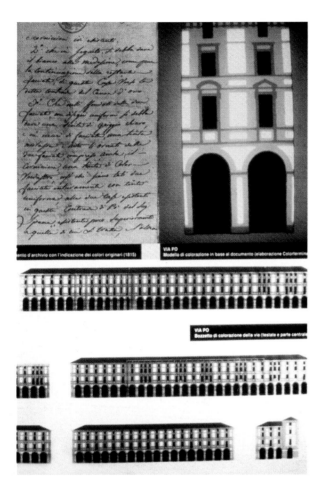

The Turin, Italy, Color Restoration Project: an archive document of the colors of Via Po, one of the main streets of the city center. (Photo: Giovanni Brino.)

At the end of 1978, Professor Brino proposed to the Municipality to set up an operational color plan for Turin, based on the critical reconstruction of the nineteenth-century plan, extended through appropriate adaptations and revisions to the whole territory of Turin. His proposal was accepted immediately, and Brino was officially designated as consultant on the coloration of the roughly 1,000 facades repainted annually. The illustrations show the methodology followed systematically for the entire city, from the identification of the archive document, to the color project, to the facade restoration of the most important streets and squares of the city.

Thanks to the incredible mass of Archive documents and projects and paintings found in the local museums, it has been possible not only to reconstruct the original "Color Map" of the city with its corresponding "Color Palette," but also to create a "Color Data Bank" in order to manage in real time the chromatic data found in the documents. For the Turin Color Plan, Giovanni Brino was awarded the 2nd prize at the "2nd International Color Design Competition."

In order to improve the quality of the facade restoration work in Turin, after 40 years of neglect in the historical city center, with the consequent lack of building maintenance, and the disappearance of the traditional materials with which the Turinese facades were originally painted (essen-

A sample facade of the same street after restoration. (Photo: Giovanni Brino.)

The Turin School of Restoration. Planning for the restoration of the facades of an arts-and-crafts villa in Turin, a project carried out in concert with the students of the School of Urban Restoration. (Photo: Giovanni Brino.)

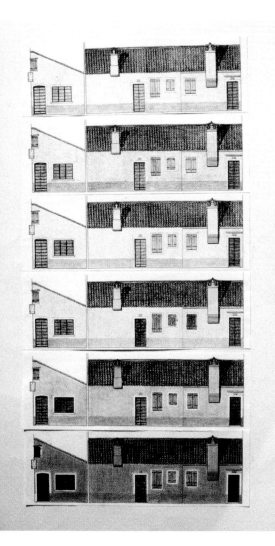

Restoration in progress on the facades of the arts-and-crafts villa. (Photo: Giovanni Brino.)

tially lime and colored pigments), a specific professional training center, The Turin School of Urban Restoration, was established by Professor Brino. In this school, professional training courses of facade restoration at an urban, regional, and Economic European Community level were organized, involving exchanges of experience with other Italian regions and other countries like France, Spain, Portugal, and Germany.

Together with this teaching and professional training activity, practical experimental work was developed with the establishment of a mobile workshop. The workshop moved easily throughout Italy and other countries and provided the opportunity to survey specific restorations in contexts different from that of Turin. The workshop has been in operation since 1983 and is staffed by a team of skilled craftsmen (masons, house painters, restorers, etc., according to the task to be confronted). It has also made it possible to carry out restoration work with traditional techniques and materials.

Through the mobile workshop it has been possible to do many facade restorations with lime colors, fresco, and tempera techniques in various Italian regions, as well as in other European and extra-European countries, in cooperation with Italian, French, Swiss, English, American, and Australian universities, using, whenever possible, specific local materials and techniques of facade decoration (e.g., frescoes, graffitoes, and trompe-l'oeil).

Restoration of a trompe-l'oeil shutter, carried out in Lugano, Italy, by students of the Southern California Institute of Architecture in cooperation with the Turin School of Urban Restoration. (Photo: Giovanni Brino.)

Painting the shutter. (Photo: Giovanni Brino.)

PART VII

Environmental Color and Light

The inspiration for environmental color art at the scale of the built environment originates in the depths of human imagination, which knows no limits. By accentuating the spatial qualities of architecture through immersing the environment in colored light, or by embedding a structure's physical attributes in a spatial layering of pigment, environmental color works today reflect a rich, varied capacity to bring new and exciting images into our world.

Preliminary color study for Valentino Village resort complex in Noci Bari, Italy. (Photo: © Brian Clarke's Studio, London.)

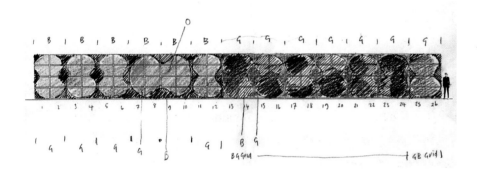

Preliminary color study for Valentino Village. (Photo: © Brian Clarke's Studio, London.)

Colored Light for Valentino Village

The 100 square meters of stained glass in the conference center and the Locale Regia Tower at the new Valentino Village complex in Noci Bari, Italy, is the work of artist Brian Clarke, in collaboration with architect Emilio Ambaz. Valentino Village is a resort village with facilities for business and conferences. Clarke's ability to link internal architectural space with external natural

"Color and architecture belong together. Even the monochromatic architecture of late Modernism derives its power from the conscious exclusion of color. Color acts as a poetic and psychological bridge between two worlds, the pragmatic and the imaginative, and by engaging the problems of the former the door to the latter can be opened. Used without a careful eye on the practical implications, color can completely transform and destroy internal space and external massing. Used in response to spatial volume and mass, it can bring architectural logic and poetic exuberance to any built structure. It is the most powerful tool in the artistic pantheon."

Brian Clarke
London, England

space through a subtle interplay of colors and transparent tones makes this area glow with exuberance and optimism. The medium used in the preliminary studies is colored pencil on paper. Larger preliminary designs were executed as acrylic collages on card stock. Brian Clarke's studio uses a variety of German stained glass studios for the production of architectural artworks in glass. The works are normally installed by these studios, or if circumstances preclude that, by local craftsmen.

Arranged in a series of carefully orchestrated stages with a field of substantial color, the stained glass, when viewed from the inside, acts like a gentle filter, allowing pools of light to fall on the floor of the conference theater. The illumination inside the room is muted, with the glass acting like a screen to the strong Mediterranean sunlight. By virtue of the transmitted light through the glass, the room is animated by swatches of color. On the outside, Clarke's composition works in two ways. At

Final color study for Valentino Village.
(Photo: © Brian Clarke's Studio, London.)

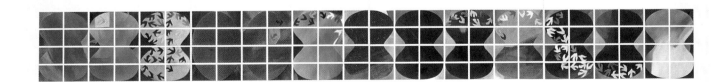

Interior view of stained glass window of
conference theater at Valentino Village. (Photo:
© Tony Shafrazi Gallery, New York.)

night, illuminated from within, the window
forms a curved, radiant colored frieze. By day,
the mixture of opaque and antique glass,
together with precise leadlines, forms an artwork which is perceived almost entirely by
reflected light. The shapes and lines of the
composition function as a blind, behind which
the activity of the theater can go on undis-
turbed by passers-by.

Exterior evening view of stained glass window of
conference theater at Valentino Village. (Photo:
© Brian Clarke's Studio, London.)

Exterior daytime view of stained glass window of
conference theater at Valentino Village. (Photo:
© Brian Clarke's Studio, London.)

"*Light is a metaphor for enlightenment. Light has always stood for the agent through which one contacts the large, natural order.*"

Charles Ross
New York, New York

Prisms

The Dwan Light Sanctuary at the Armand Hammer United World College of the American West is a collaborative project involving the solar spectrum work of Charles Ross with Virginia Dwan and architect Laban Wingert. The concept for this unique structure was born in the vision of Virginia Dwan, who imagined a space developed from the concept of the spiritual and temporal universality of the number 12. Integral to this idea was the incorporation of 12 angles of light within a circular space. Charles Ross suggested a space where the movement of the spectrum and the form of the building would act together—a space for the prisms shaped by the earth's alignment to the sun, moon, and stars. The site was selected to capitalize on the spectacular northern New Mexico light.

The orientation and geometry of the building are derived from its alignment to the sun, moon, and stars. Projecting from a circular core are two apses, each containing six large prisms mounted in sloping windows to capture light rays from sunrise to sunset. Interacting with spectrums cast from the windows are spectrums from twelve more prisms mounted in the roof that form broad ribbons of pure color. These ribbons move in concert with the rotation of the Earth. Lunar spectrums can be seen on nights when

Exterior of Dwan Light Sanctuary, Armand Hammer United World College of the West, Montezuma, New Mexico. Space and Solar Spectrum Sculpture by artist Charles Ross. (Photo: Polly Mullen.)

the moon is full. A third apse, facing north, houses a square window which frames trees and sky during the day and the North Star at night. A line parallel to the axis of the earth extends from the center of the floor through the center of the North Star window. The floor is divided into twelve segments by bronze strips that radiate from a central axis. The circular part of the building is 36 feet in diameter and reaches 23 feet in height. The floor dimensions represent solar and lunar proportions. The 24 large prisms

Detail of east apse, Dwan Light Sanctuary. The sanctuary is illuminated by 12 prisms in the apses, each 12 × 12 × 60 inches, and by 12 prisms in the skylights, each 12 × 12 × 72 inches. The interior wall of the space, a circular form, is 36 feet in diameter, and the space is 23 feet high. (Photo: Polly Mullen.)

produce orchestrated spectrum events that circulate through the space, changing by the hour and with the seasons. Conceived as a place for quiet reflection, the sanctuary was dedicated in 1996 at the United World College in Montezuma, New Mexico.

Spectrum during meditation, Dwan Light
Sanctuary. (Photo: Polly Mullen.)

Dwan Light Sanctuary.
(Photo: Polly Mullen.)

Imagery and Color Fusion

The recently opened Hodari Children's Library and Media Center at Temple Israel in West Bloomfield, Michigan, is filled with high-tech innovations, including a video reading library and a dozen or more computer terminals connected to the Internet and other synagogues around the world. As designers for this $1.8 million building expansion project at the country's largest and fastest-growing reformed Jewish synagogue, Stuart Fine, Architect, and Eugene Baker, Interior Architect, invited artist/colorist

Hodari Children's Library and Electronic Media Center is a cylindrical building addition to Temple Israel, West Bloomfield, Michigan. (Photo: Harold Linton.)

"A color consultant/designer should understand in depth his/her objectives before selecting the most appropriate color strategy for a project. I design in color in such a manner as to help an architect or interior designer gain the spatial expression he/she desires. If I am a painter, painting architecture is probably a truthful analysis of what I do, thereby acting for the architect as his/her brush and palette and helping to focus the architectural experience and fuse the building space with a visual, theoretical, and philosophical objective."

Harold Linton
Peoria, Illinois

Harold Linton to conceive the centerpiece, a new three-dimensional design of the Star of David. The vision of Eugene R. Baker and Associates in collaboration with Linton was to create an exuberant space, bright and full of energy, inviting to adults and (especially) children. The new form of the star for the ceiling of this circular room should be a vibrant symbol of the heart of Jewish history and tradition as well as an inspiration for the present and future.

Both designer and artist worked together toward the color plan for the space. Symbols of the faith were created for the interior design to appeal to children and serve as an exciting invitation to use and experience the media center. The Hebrew alphabet, a scene of Jerusalem, and two 8-foot-tall Sabbath candles—all larger than life—were planned in coordination with recessed illumination by various colored light sources which animated the color graphics and created an intriguing atmosphere around the Star of David.

One of several color sketch studies developed for the interior wall of the cylindrical room, approximately 130 feet in circumference. (Photo: Harold Linton.)

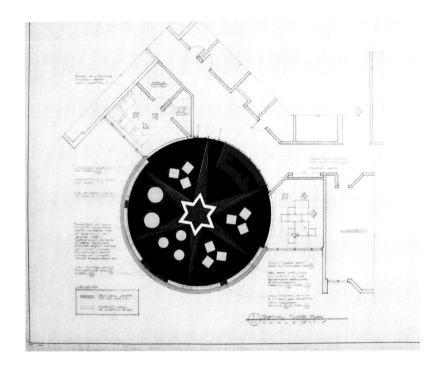

Several schemes were created for the custom carpet and floor plans for the media center. (Photo: Harold Linton.)

Color and design refinements for the three-dimensional Star of David were created on a MAC using the Clarisworks drawing program. (Photo: Harold Linton.)

Color sketch drawings of the interior design concept were generated by Baker and Associates to study the background color range and lighting effects, and to establish several nodes of contrast and points of interest around the cylindrical space. Relief studies and architectural models were created to explore the interaction of color, light, and form on the walls, ceiling, floor, and design for the star on the ceiling. Computer-generated color studies created by Linton were applied to small study model forms and eventually to three ⅓-scale maquettes. Each of these designs was viewed in relation to the design created by Baker to visualize the full impact of the concept within the space.

One of several one-third-size models of the Star of David, created to test aspects of color, light, shadow, and composition. (Photo: Harold Linton.)

The Star of David, fabricated from canvas and poplar wood and weighing 300 pounds, is suspended from a cable system attached to steel beams in the ceiling. It appears to float in space beneath the 14-foot ceiling, and its three-dimensional construction and active color-form composition shift with respect to its asymmetrical planes as one views the work from various angles around the room. The popularity of the Library and Media Center is reflected in the considerable use and attention it receives from the synagogue membership, metropolitan religious study groups, and visitors from across the country.

Hodari Children's Library and Media Center
opened in 1995. (Photo: Harold Linton.)

PART VIII

Education, Technology, and Research

Formal color education for most art, architecture, and design students usually begins in an academic or professional art and design school. The programs of the Bauhaus instructors Johannes Itten and Josef Albers are among the most common models for basic color design curricula today. Since Albers' tenure at Yale University, from 1950 to 1963, two new generations of colorists (including his students and his students' students) have distinguished themselves in the field of color education by developing and publishing their own approaches to color design, and extending, questioning, broadening, and experimenting with the lessons of Itten and Albers in aspects of dimensional thinking, graphic design, and applications for computer-aided design and visualization.

The social sciences have also played a keen role in the development of methods for the study of color and human behavior, to advance the overall quality of our environment and lives. Technology has provided the design community with sophisticated new tools for color planning and for the visualization of new environments. Planning in real time and convincingly realizable space and form allows the design professional to move closer to predicting and experiencing the design concept before it is built. These areas of inquiry and exploration, together with the growth of color education in professional design program curricula, have given rise to a new generation of architects and designers who naturally plan with color in their daily practices. Science, technology, and education have together enabled the design professions to visualize the future in both a multidimensional and multi-hued spatial experience.

To best understand the impact of various colors and building materials on the design of the entrance and facade for a new corporate headquarters for 3M Corporation in Livonia, Michigan, Architect Paul Urbanek created several preliminary color studies. (Photo: Harley Ellington Design, Southfield, Michigan.)

Color in Graphic Education

Increasing opportunities for architects and designers to work with color in a clear and creative way as part of their natural method of design are in large part due to the exposure they received during their professional education which provided early confidence and helped to eliminate apprehensions about control, graphic technique, and aesthetic direction of their work. Contributions to the growth of color in design education would certainly include highly motivating texts such as *Color Drawing* by Michael Doyle and *Drawing and Designing with Confi-*

Testing glass and panel system. (Photo: Harley
Ellington Design, Southfield, Michigan.)

dence by Mike Lin, both published in the early
1980s and growing in popularity into the 1990s.

Paul Urbanek, associated with Harley Ellington Design in Southfield, Michigan, is one
example of the growing number of young, talented architects who have benefited from the
increase in color exposure in architectural education in the 1980s and who use color with confidence in communication drawings and daily
design decision making. For a recent project for
the 3M Corporation's Automotive Industry Center in Livonia, Michigan, Urbanek used tracing

overlays on top of computer-generated wire-frame drawings to quickly visualize and compose color and design elements, including decisions about building materials, aspects of scale, and landscape and color composition. His approach toward solving the design for the entrance to the new building for 3M included manipulation of the building materials and their coloration. The challenge of a formal color design statement for the cylindrical meeting space and entry facade behind were resolved through progressive color studies created in colored pencil to test various alternatives.

Final design decision in glass. (Photo: Harley Ellington Design, Southfield, Michigan.)

Virtual Space As a Future Color Design Tool*

Virtual reality is a process whereby the viewer is immersed in a three-dimensional, synthetic computer graphics visual environment. In order to gain real-time graphics interactivity, the quality of the images is compromised due to the display speed requirements to prevent latency or "lag" of the computer graphics. The potential of virtual reality and immersion for color and architectural design is a double-edged sword. Immersing an individual in a three-dimensional virtual rendition of a proposed architectural space provides the potential for previsualizing the real-world experience. However, the primary difficulty here is the current limited quality of display devices and mechanisms for virtual reality systems.

One of the best immersive environments is the Computer Animation Video Enhanced (CAVE) system—a rear-screen, three-dimensional stereo display device. The CAVE is extremely valuable for immersive virtual experiences because the viewer steps into a stereo-viewed theater. The individual is plunged into the three-dimensionality of the synthetic computer world. Architectural spaces can be designed and then viewed from within the CAVE. The experience is profoundly better than seeing a computer graphics view on the front of a small computer screen; rather, the viewer is surrounded with a stereo view of a three-

"Virtual reality will be a color design tool of the future, but now is a challenge because VR color is not as true as it could be."

*Donna Cox, Professor of Art
University of Illinois, Urbana-
Champaign, Illinois*

* © 1998 by Donna Cox.

dimensional modeled world for a total, immersive experience.

In the illustration, Donna Cox and Robert Patterson are surrounded by CAVE walls and experience the three-dimensionality as if they were standing in a room with colliding galaxies suspended in front of them. They are the creators of the "Virtual Director," and are using this application as a "designer's workbench" for choreographing, previewing, and recording computer graphic animations. With this application, a user can use the CAVE as a previsualization tool and output camera paths to create high-resolution computer graphics animations.

The illustration shows a close-up of what users might see on the front wall of the CAVE

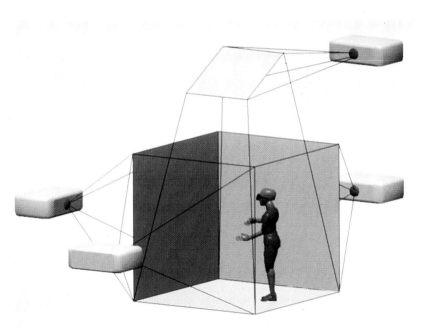

The CAVE is a 10-foot cubed rear-screen-projection stereo (three-dimensional-view) theater for immersive virtual reality experiences. The CAVE is the hardware and library that supports numerous software applications, such as the "Virtual Director." For details on the CAVE you can search for "CAVE Virtual Reality" on the Web or see http://www.graphics.stanford.edu/~comba/gccg/sig93subsection3_5_3.html. (Credit: CAVE™ Diagram copyright 1992 by Lewis Siegel and Kathy O'Keefe, Electronic Visualization Laboratory, University of Illinois at Chicago.)

Standing in the CAVE, artists Donna Cox and Robert Patterson design a three-dimensional camera path through a supercomputer simulation of colliding galaxies. The "Virtual Director" is a virtual-reality camera choreography tool for navigating, recording, and playing back animations of three-dimensional data sets. The playback is shown in the upper right television window in this figure. The "Virtual Director" is voice-driven, and the camera paths are created with motion gestures of a hand-held wand. (Credit: Donna Cox and Robert Patterson using CAVE "Virtual Director" software. This software was cocreated by Cox, Patterson, and Marcus Thiebaux. Copyright 1996, MCSA/UIUC. Photo by Jeff Carpenter, copyright NCSA/UIUC. http://www.ncsa.uiuc.edu/VR/grants/.)

while using the "Virtual Director" as a collaboration tool among several geographically remote virtual sites. The image shows how several people can share the same experience by using multiple virtual reality systems and sharing the camera data through the Internet. Each viewer

The "Virtual Director" allows users to share camera information and collaborate over long distances. The users here are represented as red smiley faces in virtual space. Bob Patterson is represented by the smiley face on the left, while Stuart Levy is in a remote virtual site, and represented on the right as a winking avatar. Donna Cox is viewing the Bob and Stuart avatars, and her viewpoint is demonstrated in this illustration. Her hand is represented as a yellow outline in the foreground of the image. Donna, Bob, and Stuart are communicating using digital audio over the network, while they share this virtual space as a visual immersive experience. Search http://www.search.hotbot.com for "Virtual Director" entries and links. (Credit: Donna Cox, Robert Patterson, Marcus Thiebaux, and Stuart Levy. Copyright NCSA/UIUC.)

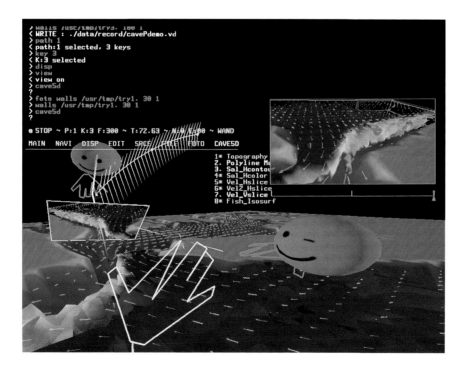

is seen as an "avatar," a symbolic incarnation of the human user in the virtual space. This remote collaborative capability of "Virtual Director" points to a future where designers will collaborate remotely over great distances while sharing the same virtual space.

The "Virtual Director" was used as a design tool to choreograph scenes for an IMAX movie, *Cosmic Voyage*, which was funded by the Smithsonian Institution and the Motorola Foundation. *Cosmic Voyage*, a large-format film about the relative scale of things in our universe, was nominated for an Academy Award in 1997. The "Virtual Director" played a major role in choreographing the film's animation scenes; however, color was designed and controlled independently of the virtual-reality system.

The primary problem with all virtual reality displays is the limited quality of color when it is viewed by the eye in the virtual space, and then translated to color in the real world or to other media. In CAVE, color is rear-projected onto screens using video projectors. The video projectors are controlled by a Silicon Graphics Onyx Reality engine. The color is created by using software such as Alias or by programming OpenGL. CAVEs and their less expensive virtual reality versions all need calibration and maintenance for power stereo projection and color. Yet even with the most advanced calibration systems, color is never as true as it should be. Part of the problem is that virtual-reality projection systems to date are not bright enough; they tend to be dark to help create the illusion of the space; and any excess light interferes with the illusion of the virtual set. Light spills from one wall of the CAVE to other parts of the display and dilutes color saturation and intensity. Such issues can compromise the quality of experience. Future display screens and panels will certainly improve the quality of color.

For now, however, the design process must accommodate for disparity between color experienced in virtual reality and that translated to various media. The challenge is to make the immersive experience translate into a viable, comparable, and desirable real-world experience whether the output is color on walls of an architectural building or textures on synthetic walls of a computer animation. The current solution is to readjust color as it is being transferred to the final medium. For example, color is often postprocessed for visual accuracy before being rendered to animation videos. Gamma, intensity, and hue can be readjusted as a separate step in the process of making a video or movie. As the technology advances and display devices provide a sharper, clearer image with crisp, bright color, then one can expect that virtual reality will become a better tool for the color designer.

Simulating Real-World Complexity

To facilitate the use of color in architectural design it is necessary to improve the methods and instruments for exploring and communicating color during the design process. Architectural design visualization and simulation are central instruments of the architectural design process. To determine their quality and applicability in architectural color design, the psychological effectiveness of different simulation techniques has to be evaluated and compared.

Working with students of architecture at the Department for Spatial Simulation at the Vienna University of Technology in 1995–1996, Dr. Leonhard Oberascher carried out five projects in which the appearance, effect, meaning, and functions of color in architectural space were explored experimentally by using and comparing different techniques of project visualization and spatial simulation. In particular, Dr. Oberascher was interested in comparing the effectiveness and applicability of full-scale modeling versus other techniques of spatial simulation, project visualization, and documentation.

The experiments suggest that full-scale modeling is the most appropriate method and medium to explore, assess, and communicate the appearance, the impact, and the cognitive, emotional, and behavioral effects that color will have in a completed architectural space.

Introduction

The architectural design process mediates the translation of conceptual ideas into physical

"The effect of color in the context of man-made environments is perceived within the parameters of space and time, material and form, light and surface, as well as movement, action, characteristics, and state of mind of the people using them. In general, it is difficult to assess and predict during the design process how these factors will influence each other in a completed architectural space. Full-scale modeling of color in 3-D offers architects and designers a promising instrument for experimental exploration of new color design concepts, affording them more insight into how these factors interact and contribute to the overall color impression in the completed architectural space."

Leonhard Oberascher
Salzburg, Austria

reality. It involves the anticipation and communication of physically nonexistent structures, their form, function, and impact. Different methods of project visualization allow the creation of stand-ins for reality, which help to explore, assess, and communicate the different design elements, their roles, their impact on each other and on the entire physical structure, and how these factors could influence the observer's cognitive, emotional, and behavioral responses.

Most of the design visualization methods incorporate the possibility of color representation and manipulation. Nevertheless, it is difficult to accurately predict the actual appearance, impact, and effects of color in the completed architectural space; this may be one of the reasons why the role of color in architectural design is often neglected.

Assessing and Predicting the Appearance, Impact, and Psychological Effects of Color in the Architectural Space

The general task in architectural color design is to bring the functions of color (indicative, symbolic, aesthetic)[1] into accord with the functions to be fulfilled by the space or elements of that space. During the successive phases of the design process the architect will be confronted with the following questions: To what extent can color support the functions of the space? Which color design concept is the most suitable? What will it look like? How will the observer/user respond to it?

The architect's conclusions in response to these questions are based on a combination of previous experience, empirical generalizations, design assessment, evaluation, and mere speculation. He or she cannot be sure that these conclusions were correct, however, until the project is completed. As Schreibmayer[2] remarks, the architect might well be wrong: "Our environment is disfigured with buildings that might have been well meant but in fact were major mistakes; they are constructed errors, since this very conclusion is often . . . made [only] when the structure is finished."

However, with regard to architectural color design, not all the blame can be put on the architect alone. One has to acknowledge that predicting the appearance, impact, and cognitive, emotional, and behavioral effects that color will have in a completed architectural space is indeed not a straightforward task.

Appearance and Impact of Color in Architectural Space

Color in the architectural context is not a simple perceptual entity. It is perceived within the parameters of space, time, movement, and environmental changes. The color image of the architectural space is generated by integrating sequential perceptions of individual scenes into a coherent whole. The color impressions evoked by the individual scenes are in themselves the result of the compound effects of various factors:

• Space-establishing elements (planes, bodies, and structures) are arranged in such a way that they define subspaces and influence each other's appearance.

- They consist of different materials with different properties (e.g., surface, texture, pattern and structure, transmission, reflection, and spectral properties) that influence their color appearance.
- They are illuminated by natural light and different sources of artificial light which determine their own color and affect the color appearance of the other elements in the space.
- The quality and composition of the illumination differ according to its spatial distribution, and they change through time.
- The illuminated elements modify the illumination of the space and other elements by absorbing, reflecting, or transmitting portions of the light.
- The elements and the conditions of illumination are seen partly simultaneously, partly in a sequential order, depending on the viewpoint and movement of the observer.
- Through the movement of the observer, a gradual transition of the perceived scene takes place. The perceived fragments of the space are organized and stored in the observer's short- and long-term memory. They are combined with the actual impression of space to create and maintain a coherent image of the whole architectural space.

The mutual interdependence of color with other environmental qualities, as well as the conceptual confounding of these variables, contributes to the problem of assessing and predicting the appearance, impact, and psychological effects of color in architectural design.

Assessing Total Color Appearance

Elementary color attributes, as for example used in the NCS, are meant to describe the appearance of uniformly colored surfaces only.[3] Despite this restriction in design practice, the NCS notations have proved to be quite helpful in describing the dominant color impression of multicolored and structured surfaces or even transparent materials, but they tell us nothing about any other visual quality.

Jose Luis Caivano[4] points out that color theory has been evoked by some researchers to consider factors such as transparency, brightness, opacity, and so forth, but so far no color order system has been developed to include these factors. Based on Cesar Janello's concept of *cesia*,* he suggests a model which allows the specification of visual sensations that depend on the spatial distribution of light—such as transparency, specular reflection, translucence, diffuse reflection and absorption (black). Caivano demonstrates convincingly that it is possible to organize the "geometric attributes of appearance" in a

---

* In the absence of any generic term for phenomena that are independent of but related to color, Janello coined the new word *cesia,* which he derived from his own name Cesar. Cesia refers to perception arising from differences in the spatial distribution of light excluding texture.[4]

three-dimensional coordinate system and to produce scales of these attributes by synthetic
means.* He concludes that "it is not impossible
to build an atlas of cesias which can serve for the
visual comparison of any sample of material."

Paul Green-Armitage[6] draws attention to the
insufficiency of the color vocabulary and argues
for the necessity to develop an extended taxo-
nomic framework which will incorporate other
visual qualities that are distinct from color but at
the same time inseparable from it—such as texture, gloss, and transparency. He proposes to
use the heraldic term *tincture* to describe elements beyond but including color. With reference to the work of Cesar Janello, Claudio
Guerri, and Jose Caivano, he suggests a system
of tinctures which "accommodate such scales as
matt to glossy, glossy to metallic, transparent to
opaque, smooth to rough, as well as scales connecting the so-called modes of appearance: illu-
minate, illumination, surface, volume and film."[6]

But probably still more factors need to be
considered and included if the concept of tincture is to fulfill the conditions for describing "all
aspects of what we see beyond but including

* Similar to Maxwell's method of additive color mixture, the relative amount of stimuli that cause primary
sensations of cesia are varied on a spinning disc in
such a manner that perceptually equal intervals are
generated. The different scales can be organized in a
coordinate system based on the dimensions of absorption, permeability, and diversity. If a different solid
were made for each different hue and saturation, any
cesia a color may be could be equally defined.[5]

colour." A complete system of tinctures would definitely also have to include scales of iridescence. One could think of constructing a scale from noniridescent to iridescent for each hue and saturation, and then combining it with the five primary sensations of cesia.

Another dimension which requires consideration is *micropolychromy*.[7] This dimension would consist of several scales, including a scale from dichromatic to polychromatic, and scales defining the relationship between the color elements (e.g., contrast of hue, chromaticity, and lightness). Micropolychromy is an important feature of many building materials, such as laminates, solid-surface materials, or floor coverings. From a suitable viewing distance they appear as a homogeneous surface, but nevertheless their color appearance will always be distinct from a comparable plain-colored surface. In the natural environment, plain-colored surfaces in a strict sense do not exist. In most of the surfaces we distinguish more than one color. We may call a stone gray, but we cannot describe its grayness unless we say it is a stone. The concept "stone" obviously contains much more information about its total color appearance than we could probably ever communicate by a system of tinctures. Some architects, for example, are convinced that a color concept can easily be replaced by a material concept—but not vice versa.

The conceptual separation of color (together with cesia, texture, and other factors that contribute to total color appearance) from its environmental context (e.g., object, material, space and time, function and meaning) requires a high degree of abstraction which is far from representing the reality. But architectural design means creating "new" realities that have function and meaning, evoke emotions, involve cognition and structure behavior.

John Hutchings[8,9] presents a model for assessing complex visual scenes, taking into consideration also the emotional, cognitive, and behavioral aspects of appearance. He points out that if one wishes to understand the formation and impact of appearance images, it is necessary to analyze both the properties of a scene and the characteristics of the perceiver. The effectiveness or preference of a scene results from "a personal opinion of quality." The hedonic judgment of a scene includes initial opinions about the "overall suitability of the object for the purpose [for which] it was required," or "the overall degree of acceptability or beauty of the scene," as well as more detailed sensory, emotional, and intellectual judgments that are made once the viewer has become involved in the scene. Inherited and learned responses, individual receptor mechanisms, and immediate environmental factors (geographical, social, medical) influence the judgments of the perceiver. Assessment of the scene can be carried out by instrumental measurement, sensory assessment, or by an overall quality judgment (connotation) "by looking directly at the whole, or by taking it apart, examining the pieces and reassembling the whole while considering their interactions." The factors affecting Total Appearance can be listed in a logical manner and applied to the analysis of real scenes. The concept does not claim to give a final solution to the problems of design and image, but to "provide a methodology for thinking about the disciplined control of the images we create and those to which we are subjected."

Predictive Environmental Assessment

With the idea that psychological assessment techniques—originally used to assess persons—may be applied to the assessment of physical settings under the term *Environmental Assessment*, Craik[10] suggests ". . . a general conceptual and methodological framework for describing and predicting how attributes of places* relate to a wide range of cognitive, affective, and behavioural responses." One important concern of Environmental Assessment is to establish dependable predictive relations between descriptive attributes of places and how they are evaluated and used, with the hope that this will advance ". . . our understanding of environment-behaviour transactions and [afford] the basis for improving the planning, design, and management of our environment." Dependable predictive relations between descriptive attributes of places and how they are evaluated and used can be derived either on the basis of empirical generalizations or environmental simulations.[11]

In the field of architecture and design, simulation techniques have been used for many centuries.[12,13,14] Beside traditional forms of project visualization and simulation, advanced simulation technologies offer a broad palette of sophisticated tools for professional communication and

* The term *place* is used as a general designation for an environmental display or environmental unit.[10]

decision making. Central to the use of any simulation-based predictions is the question as to whether the responses to the simulation accurately predict responses to real-world settings.

At the Department for Spatial Simulation at the Vienna University of Technology, students and professionals have the opportunity to use and compare different simulation techniques. Besides the possibilities of computer-aided design (e.g., CAD, CAAD, CAI), model endoscopy, stereophotography, and holography, the department has installed an experimental laboratory for full-scale modeling.[15] In 1995–1996, in collaboration with students of architecture, we carried out five projects in which the appearance, effect, meaning, and functions of color in architectural space were explored experimentally by using and comparing different techniques of project visualization and spatial simulation. In particular, we were interested in comparing the effectiveness and applicability of full-scale modeling* versus other techniques of

* According to Craik: "Full-scale mock-up versions of proposed environments fall between the categories of actual environments and simulations. However, because they occur in laboratory or temporary contexts and may not be fully detailed in their materials, their use raises the same issues of descriptive, evaluative, and behavioral comparability as those generated by applications of [other] perceptual forms of environmental simulations [. . .]. Furthermore their full-scale, three-dimensional character opens up interesting possibilities for extending the study of behavioral equivalence between simulated and ordinary-use environments."[10]

spatial simulation and project visualization and documentation.

Procedure

1. Prior to design, quality criteria (e.g., "legibility," "security," "directing movement") for each architectural setting were set up and their meaning clarified.
2. Descriptive attributes predominantly related to color appearance and considered relevant to the architectural setting were identified and further specified with regard to the quality criteria. It was assumed they would predict emotional, cognitive, and behavioral responses to the architectural setting (e.g., "only specific hue contrasts will facilitate legibility").
3. During the successive phases of the design process, evaluations of the architectural setting presented via different simulation techniques were carried out. The relations between predominantly color-appearance attributes and quality criteria were experimentally tested, corrected, or optimized (e.g., "only specific hue contrasts will facilitate legibility").
4. After the completion of the full-scale model, the architectural setting was individually evaluated with regard to the quality criteria. The evaluation included cognitive, emotional, and behavioral responses: "Is the organization of the space easy to understand?" "Do I feel in control of the space?" "Is it easy for me to move around within the space?"

5. The individual responses to the full-scale model were summarized and compared with the initial assumptions and evaluations made under conditions of simulation similar to the full-scale model.

6. Evaluations of the architectural setting presented via different full-scale model documentation techniques were carried out and compared with the reactions to the full-scale model (e.g., "Are responses to documentations of the full-scale model the same as to the full-scale model?").

General Results

During the planning, simulation, and evaluation of these projects it became evident that compared to full-scale modeling, none of the other simulation techniques used (colored perspectives, colored scale models, scale-model photography, color and material samples, computer-aided simulation, photography, stereophotography, and video presentation of the full-scale model) allows a better prediction of the actual appearance, impact of, and responses to color in the completed architectural space. Many of the effects caused by the complex (and sometimes subtle) interactions between color and other environmental variables can be presented, experienced, and assessed only by means of full-scale modeling. Several times we noticed that even small changes in one environmental variable can cause completely unexpected changes in the whole setting. It also became evident that certain color effects (e.g., simultaneous contrast

Simulation technique effectiveness studies at the
Department for Spatial Simulation, Vienna University of
Technology. Here, a project designed to create a continuous
transition between the states of chromaticity and
achromaticity. The space consisted of two concentric
cylinders, with the inner one covered by white cloth and
fixed in place, and the outer one, revolving, consisting partly
of colorless transparent material, partly of translucent
sections of various colors. The speed of rotation,
translucency of the materials, and angle of incidence,
distribution, intensity, and color of the light determined the
overall color impression in the inner cylinder. In the
photograph above, students try to estimate the probable
color/space effect with the help of an endoscope, using a
1:20 model. At upper right, a student in the 1:1 model
observes the continually changing situation and describes
his momentary impressions to colleagues standing outside
the model. The view at right shows the completed 1:1
model from the outside. The color effect of the space could
be only very approximately predicted from the 1:20 model.
It was only in the 1:1 simulation that the complex
combination of movement, light, and combinations of
space/material and surface/texture and color could be
replicated. (Photos: Dr. Leonhard Oberascher.)

effects, illumination effects) which were seen under the condition of full-scale modeling could be neither simulated nor reproduced by other means of documentation such as videotaping or photographic or stereophotographic representation of the full-scale model.

Comparing the Effectiveness and Applicability of Full-Scale Modeling versus Other Simulation Techniques

Perceptual Quality. Despite the fact that color is a visual phenomenon, the actual color appearance of the architectural space in the full-scale modeling situation could not be adequately simulated by any of the other simulation techniques.

As described previously, color appearance in the architectural context is the result of the compound effects of various factors, including time, movement, and environmental changes, as well as the active engagement of the viewer. Some problems of simulating color can be related to the question of scale: "Color cannot be scaled down," is a comment often made by architects. Obviously they do not mean color as such, but other factors such as texture, cesia, and micropolychromy, which are typical for the appearance of many building materials. Other problems of simulating color can be related to the question of illumination: Computer-generated images, for example, often look very impressive as regards illumination effects, especially if the scene includes glossy and metallic materials. However, the interactive effects often given by color reflex lights in a

These illustrations show a project in which the formal aesthetic effect of color in an architectural context was examined by experiment. The 1:1 model consisted of a plain white room in which various geometric elements were positioned. These elements were interchangeable and could also be independently lighted. This enabled variation of the color of both objects and light. Attention was focused upon how far the effect of the design determined by the form and arrangement of the objects could be influenced in relation to the dimensions of "light-heavy," "open-closed," "stable-unstable" by changes in color, light, texture, and pattern. Also, in this project the students learned by experience that the complex interaction of these factors and their influence on the overall color effect could be perceived and assessed only using the 1:1 model. (Photos: Dr. Leonhard Oberascher.)

simple space on matte surfaces seem to go beyond the possibilities of computer simulation, and cannot be adequately simulated in a scale model.

Cognitive Quality.   Despite the fact that attributes predominantly related to color appearance considered relevant to the architectural setting were identified prior to (and further specified during) the design process, their mutual interdependence and their relation to and impact on the scene were not completely understood under any simulation condition other than full-scale modeling.

Emotional Quality.   Despite the fact that color is a visual phenomenon, the emotional effect caused by the color appearance of the architectural space in the full-scale modeling situation could not be adequately evoked through other simulation techniques. The emotions evoked by the colors of a space (or elements in a space) depend to a great extent upon the observer's degree of physical involvement in the setting. For example, the feeling of security caused by "being surrounded by warm soft-looking earth colors" in the full-scale modeling situation could be imagined but not experienced under other simulation conditions.

Behavioral Quality.   The behavioral responses caused by the color appearance of the architectural space in the full-scale modeling situation could not be adequately predicted on the basis of the other simulation techniques. Simulation

These illustrations show a project designed primarily to examine the psychological effect of color in the architectural context. Four different architectural settings were simulated and tested successively. One room was accessible only from darkness through a narrow vertical shaft 5 meters in height (above). After climbing through the shaft, the unprepared visitor was confronted with a room offering a variety of exits. Attention was focused upon which exit was chosen, and how far this choice was influenced by color design.

The illustration at upper right shows a room in which the extent of visual stimulation was varied by means of light and color. In the middle of the room hung an "escape shaft," into which the visitor could put his head in order to escape from the visual chaos. (Photos: Dr. Leonhard Oberascher.)

techniques other than full-scale modeling do not allow physical interaction with the simulated space. Behavioral reactions to the real environment can only be imagined. Under full-scale modeling conditions the behavioral effectiveness of architectural space can be empirically tested. The aim of one of the five projects was to use color to counteract the function of the space, making the comprehension and use of the space difficult or almost impossible. When Dr. Oberascher walked through the full-scale model, the misleading "affordances" communicated by the color design "caused me to fall down a staircase. The students interpreted my behavioral reaction as an explicit positive quality judgment of their work. However, I prefer to take it as an indicator for the behavioral effectiveness of full-scale color simulation."

A definite advantage of full-scale modeling over other simulation techniques is that it permits realistic physical interaction between the user and the space. The results of experiments in full-scale modeling situations demonstrate that the effect of color in an architectural contest not only depends on objective factors, but is also decisively influenced by the manner and intensity of the interaction as well as by the characteristics and state of mind of the user.

In the photograph at upper left, the basic equipment of 1:1 experimental spatial simulation includes plastic blocks which can readily be used to construct any desired architectural space. Since the color of these blocks cannot be changed, they have to be covered with other materials.

The second photo (upper right) shows a section of the complete staircase model. In comparison with the visual qualities of form and space in Illustration II, the change in surface color effected by lighting becomes clearly visible. Representation of the interaction of light, basic color, and surface color arising in a completed space is hardly feasible by means of any other simulation technique.

The third photo (lower left) shows a staircase arrangement constructed of blocks and covered with chipboard. The aim of the project was to use color contrary to the geometry and the function of the space, to make it as difficult as possible to use.

In the last photo, a half-completed 1:1 model, niches not directly in the observer's line of vision are painted in strong, bright colors and white light is directed into them. The wall panels, standing in a row, are painted in pastel colors. The effective color of the walls is determined by the mixture of surface color, color of light, and overlying reflected light. (Photos: Dr. Leonhard Oberascher.)

Conclusions

1. Environmental Assessment provides a general conceptual and methodological framework which can be adapted to empirical study of the problems of evaluation, description, and most of all prediction of real-world color appearance in architectural design.

2. Our experiments at the Department for Spatial Simulation suggest that full-scale modeling is the most appropriate method and medium for exploring, assessing, and communicating the appearance, effect, meaning, and functions of color (including its complex interactions with other variables) in architectural space.

3. The concepts of *cesia, tincture,* and *total appearance* may aid the logical understanding of such complex interactions.

   a. The concept of *cesia* concerns the relationship between color and other perceptual qualities caused by the spatial distribution of light, which contribute to its appearance but are independent of it. Although an atlas of cesias does not yet exist, the concept may serve as a notational system for specifying and describing the appearance of objects in terms of their resemblance to the five primary sensations of cesia with or without consideration of its color.

   b. The concept of *tincture* draws attention to the fact that in addition to cesia and texture there are other factors closely related to color appearance. However, a system of tinctures needs further elaboration. In particular, it would have to include iridescence and *micropolychromy*.

   c. The Total Appearance model provides an interactional approach to analyzing complex scenes. It draws attention to factors other than those directly linked to color appearance. In particular, it emphasizes the role of the perceiver. *

* Acknowledgments: Our thanks to Akzo Nobel/Sikkens Ges.m.b.H., Philips Licht GmbH, M. Kaindl/Kronospan, Leube Baustoffe, for their assistance in realizing the full-scale models.

Full-Scale Experimental Laboratory

Introduction

The full-scale laboratory is situated in the main building of the Vienna University of Technology (1816–1818) at Karlsplatz. The facilities available to the lab are directly adjacent to the centrally located first courtyard and are accessible on the ground floor via the courtyard through the main entrance. Further linkages are located in the basement and also lead directly to the stage area. By an Act of the Ministry of Science and Research on April 4, 1991, an individual Department for Spatial Simulation was installed, as the full-scale laboratory is to be regarded as an independent entity.

What Is Full-Scale Modeling?

As far as the major part of the present-day representations are concerned, the abstraction of architectural space tends to be depicted by means of ground plan, section, and view. In the case of missing experience data, the syntheses of these two-dimensional representations are hardly to be recognized in their correspondence to the three-dimensional reality. On account of this fact, the realization of exact representations of space available corresponding to the built reality is often not come up with. The characteristics of a full-scale model are still a realistic, but simpler (respectively abstract) representation of the reality to be built. Several spatial experiments seem to lend themselves particularly well to a 1:1 model representation:

- Individual units, such as hotel rooms (multipliers)
- Prototypes, when only limited space is available
- Testing of minimum dimensions (e.g., sanitary facilities)
- Fair stalls and exhibition buildings
- (Artistic) spatial installations
- Testing of intended optical illusions
- Construction projects with no relevant experience data, etc.

This listing is not to be regarded as complete. Additions to it will result from respective technical equipment and working plan of the specific laboratory. A spatial situation can be compared "before" and "after" for evaluation purposes. Two versions of a hotel room could be built next to each other for comparison.

What Is a Full-Scale Laboratory?

Many facilities, both on the inside and on the outside, could be described as "full-scale laboratories." Dealing with in-situ experiments, the main aim is to erect a (part-) model in full scale (e.g., a section of a facade) and to examine its effect within its future spatial surroundings. This procedure may lead to further improvements which, if possible, are to be depicted directly in the 1:1 model. As soon as actual building construction is ready to commence, the 1:1 model is removed. In situ model work of this kind is of inferior importance, as constructional realization of the study projects is not usually intended to be within the scope of one's studies.

But, so that not only "paper-architecture" is created during the studies, model work in full scale in laboratory conditions could represent an alternative. Under such conditions the future situation is not taken into account in the simulation process, and thus work in the laboratory is always dealing with different experiments. In practical work the presence of appropriate basic equipment or the technical infrastructure has to be taken into consideration in this context, as otherwise too much working capacity would have to be applied for the erection of auxiliary constructions.

Technical Equipment of the Laboratory

The experimental area of the laboratory on the ground floor is surrounded by an open-vault working gallery. One can watch any ongoing experiments both from this gallery and from the working area on the ground floor. The experimental stage has a clear height of practically 9 meters and a working area of approximately 60 square meters. The experimental floor and the ceiling consist of adjustable girders and floor units, providing for alterations of the floor area in any desired manner (e.g., a slanting plane). The paneling for the side walls consists of the same wood sheets as the floor units, so that operations like screwing and nailing can be easily accomplished, in a fashion similar to work on a theatrical stage. At the half-height of the room the removable banister for the working gallery becomes visible. The movable working platform has not been designed only for observation purposes. It is supposed to be used for experimental work, too—such as for suspending or positioning lightweight building members, or for the operation of the lighting fixtures in the busbars provided.

To Build with Bricks, Blocks, or Panels?

Building systems for the erection of positions can be divided into two main groups: clamped-joint panels, and building bricks or blocks. A fact to be taken into account is that sometimes considerable restrictions arise from the use of one system, when all configurations deviating from the orthogonal (e.g., slanted walls, planes, and roundings) are practically impossible.

Clamped-joint panels are wall-like elements which are clamped between floor and ceiling in a vertical direction. The particular arrangement chosen makes for a spatial termination. The width of the individual clamped-joint panels may be 30, 50, 60, 70, or 90 centimeters; and door and window elements with inset parapets have also been developed. The set room height does not really prove satisfactory for projects not within the field of residential building. Despite this limitation, a ground plan can be reconstructed with ease.

Building bricks or building blocks represent small-unit elements which can be used to reproduce building parts of various dimensions. Assembly and dismantling is not accomplished as quickly as with clamped-joint panels. Panel-like working means, however, are to be sawed into pieces and assembled according to desired size:

- In Bologna, building blocks of very sophisticated design were developed for the full-scale lab "Oikos." Individual blocks are connected by means of a special wrench. Three basic types—with the dimensions $10 \times 30 \times 10$ centimeters, $30 \times 30 \times 10$ centimeters, and $10 \times 10 \times 10$ centimeters, as well as corner elements (modifications of $10 \times 30 \times 10$ centimeters)—are at their disposal.

- The full-scale lab of the ETH-Lausanne (LEA) has developed cream-colored, injection-molded building bricks for teaching and research purposes. As of now three different types exist: a rectangular one ($20 \times 10 \times 10$ centimeters), a cubical one ($10 \times 10 \times 10$ centimeters), and one rounded on one side (for the erection of curved walls).

- "Brik" building bricks, developed in the Netherlands, though not within the 1:1 lab structure, are an alternative to the Swiss product. These patented building bricks—looking like overdimensioned Lego building bricks at first sight—are produced under license in the United States. So far, two types are available ($20 \times 10 \times 10$ centimeters and $10 \times 10 \times 20$ centimeters), which can be connected by means of connector pins. Thus overspans and cantilevers can be accomplished.

Simulation-Aided Architectural Design (SAAD)

The term SAAD refers to the implementation of spatial simulation techniques in the course of the architectural drafting. Solutions are achieved by alternative or additional means. Thus SAAD is to be regarded as a design strategy, not discarding other working modes entirely, but in addition to them also promoting the integration of traditional and newly developed representation techniques. On account of this, spatial simulation in architecture makes sense without being an end in itself.

A field of application of SAAD of preeminent importance deals with the production of design-accompanying intermediate products using the technology as design-supporting checking tool. Prototyping and modeling represent necessary working steps within the design activities in order to be able to check the reproduction and the industrial execution of a planned building. The virtual-digital and physical-analogue working levels also play an important role in this context. The analogue (working) model in its "primitive" form will influence the creative process. The virtual model in larger dimensions also distinguishes itself by being "environmentally beneficial" (as not built). Computer-aided techniques have been predominately used so far for the "imitation" of traditional working techniques.

The simulation-environment of a building within a full-scale lab is definitely to be considered as a "large-scale appliance" in terms of spatial and infrastructural equipment, requiring, however, for the major part only one-time investments. The specific prevalent situation will determine the possibilities for further development. As soon as basic laboratory equipment is provided, the stepwise extension not only becomes feasible, but frequently also very meaningful. As a further consequence, for example, the combination of Virtual Reality and the real-picture fade-in, respectively, may be envisaged.

Full-Scale Modeling and Other Types of Environmental Simulation

Full-scale modeling is not treated in an isolated manner, but principally within its context to other simulation techniques, such as VR/CAD, endoscopy, holography, and stereoscopy, as described below:

- First, computer-aided spatial simulation, with the computer acting as a kind of "electronic drawing board." By means of various two- and three-dimensional geometrical tools (lines, progressions, circles, triangles, extrusion specimens, etc.), the objects described in the design, such as walls, floors, and ceilings, are first defined in the X, Y, Z system of coordinates. Already defined objects can be changed, multiplied, or shifted as required; and several representations from various stations, with different angles of view, do not result in additional input work. A quick perspective control of the objects entered is thus easily achieved. Sophisticated programs with photorealistic rendering can make pictures that are virtually indistinguishable from real photographs. Data input can be very time-costly, however, as an exact input is necessary from the beginning. Depending on the specific requirements (e.g., realistic materials and color effects), not only are accordingly high investments necessary, but also intensive initial training; and constant practice and further education are inevitable.
- Second, stereoscopic spatial simulation, meaning that technique producing two separate images of an object (e.g., a room), which then

can be viewed together to provide the illusion of depth. The necessity for two pictures is self-explanatory when considering that two eyes are also required in the human process of depth perception. Two retina pictures are produced which merge to spatial vision. Compared with "monophotography," stereophotography makes for an increase of spatial effect. Therefore, stereoscopy can be regarded as particularly well-suited for the documentation and description of building substance and not only as an aid for interactive design work. Any model at your disposal—either in physical or digital form—can be recorded by means of stereoscopy. Physical models are inclined to get damaged and therefore rarely lend themselves to preservation for long periods of time. As 1:1 simulation will have to be dismantled at some time, stereoscopic recording will prove meaningful with regard to conservation of the specific findings in their three-dimensionality.

- Third, holographic spatial simulation. This technique enables us to store spatial objects while maintaining their three-dimensional quality. Holograms offer a new perspective when the angle of view is changed, and back parts of the picture are more or less to be seen. The original color and material effect, however, are lost. Holography seems mystically veiled—which is not justified, even though the conditions for taking holographic pictures are completely different than those governing conventional photographic procedures:

1. Either the holographic picture works out well, or it is a complete failure.

2. Blurred holograms do not exist.
3. Representation scale is 1:1 and cannot be varied.

As with stereoscopy, holography can be applied both to physical and digital models, with special regard to long-term conservation. The size restrictions encountered when dealing with holographic pictures of physical objects must, however, be accounted for. Even though it is possible to achieve a different perspective by changing one's angle of view while looking at the hologram, a single picture normally is not sufficient to provide an impression of the object in its entirety. Doubtlessly, very impressive effects can be achieved using holography, such as the representation of spatial objects which seem optically to be leaving the focal plane. In this context, however, the question as to meaningfulness of such effects arises (i.e., whether this particular holographic technique is to be used as an architect's tool in the course of design work).

- Fourth, endoscopic spatial simulation. By means of an endoscope, scaled-down models can be regarded in such a way that images from the perspective of a pedestrian result. The rigid endoscope is connected via an adapter with a CCD video camera, in order to furnish picture sequences in addition to still pictures. Unlike computer-aided spatial simulation, video-endoscopic model animation is relatively easily arrived at. Moreover, practically no initial training is required to obtain presentable results. If a model exists, it can be subjected to endoscopy without much effort.

Only in such cases as for interior rooms may some adjustments become necessary in order to render that portion of the model accessible to endoscopy. Even with models in an urban planning scale (1:500), a practically authentic description is achieved. Endoscopic pictures match the built reality more precisely than photographic pictures taken by wide-angle or fisheye lenses. An endoscope without peripheral equipment is sufficient for individual viewing, but as soon as the spatial impressions are to be stored by some means it becomes more costly. The prospect of trolling through a project is fascinating. When doing this, a special mechanism would be necessary to drive the endoscope through the model at exactly the required speed, and simultaneously check the angles of view.

The combined use of different simulation techniques will probably increase significantly in the near future. A three-dimensional computer model of the 1:1 experimental area in the full-scale lab is to be regarded as an important contribution in this respect. The digital model can then be used for the preparation of 1:1 simulations. A 1:50 model of the full-scale lab can also be used as a vicinity model for endoscopic purposes.

Master of Arts Degree Program in Color Design at the University of Art and Design, Helsinki, Finland

Being the largest and most diversified design school in Scandinavia, with 1500 students, 400 teachers, and 12 degree programs covering the entire design spectrum, the University of Art and Design Helsinki (UIAH) provides an ideal background and support for the study of color, which by nature is highly interdisciplinary. The Department of Art (the former Faculty of General Studies) at UIAH has been provided with considerable resources for developing its color teaching program over the last few years. One milestone in this work was the International Conference on Colour Education, organized and hosted by UIAH in August 1994. Another important step was the decision to allocate the department's professional chair to the area of color. This was quite momentous in the university, since among the staff of about 400 teachers, the professors, who have the highest academic status, number seven in all. At the moment the department has five faculty members devoted to the teaching of color. Professor Harold Linton from the United States served for the 1996–1997 academic year as the first professor in this area to help plan and implement the program. He is the author of several books on color and design and is recognized as a strong proponent of color design education.

Considerable material resources have also recently been invested in the area of color. For teaching and research purposes, the department has instruments for measuring spectral distribution of surface colors, luminance and chromaticity of surfaces and light sources, as well as illuminance, chromaticity, and color temperature of incident light. It also has NCS and Munsell color collections and the beginning of a teaching collection of original and printed works donated to the Color Archive Collection by professionals in color from all over the world. The vision of this collection is to serve as a professional resource and source of inspiration for students to explore the work of many well-known contemporary color designers from various professions. The latest investment is a light source comparison laboratory, which was built as an addition to the color teaching studio. This equipment is spe-

Students in the color program at the University of Art and Design, Helsinki, Finland, have a wide variety of color source and technical equipment to use during their work. (Photo: Harald Arnkil, Department of Art, UIAH.)

cially designed for demonstrating the effect of different light sources, from incandescent to fluorescent to other gas-discharge lamps, on the visual appearance of surface colors. The year 1999 will mark the inauguration of the university's new Audiovisual Center, housing a full-scale professional-quality film studio with cinema cutting, editing, and viewing rooms, and (most important for the M.A. color course) a new stage design studio/auditorium, where experiments and demonstrations with artificial interior lighting can also be carried out in 1:1 scale.

The two-year M.A. degree program in color design at UIAH was initiated in the autumn of 1996. It is the first graduate program of its kind in Europe to provide an academic opportunity

A new light booth for testing industrial light sources on various design materials as well as three-dimensional study forms is housed in the color study room. (Photo: Harald Arnkil, Department of Art, UIAH.)

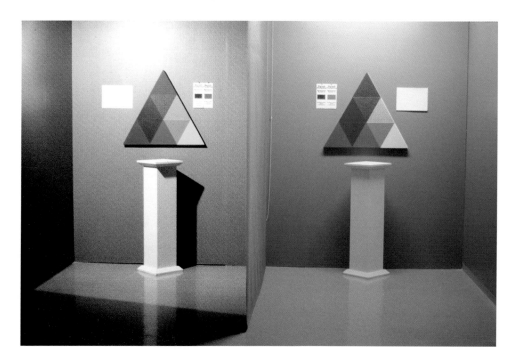

for students to specialize as color designers. The objective is to give students an artistic, theoretical, and practical knowledge of color and light applicable to fine art and design. The program is comprehensive in its reflection of an international color perspective while being rooted in the color tradition of Finland, Scandinavia, and Europe.

The program is intended for students with prior professional training, such as a B.A. or equivalent first degree in fine art, design, or architecture, and provides a specialization in

Students have access to a complete range of printed color papers to use during their coursework in the color study room. (Photo: Harald Arnkil, Department of Art, UIAH.)

color that will extend their professional opportunities. Although the degree aims at a clear professional identity, its curriculum is broad in academic preparation. The studies include interaction of color, color classification and identification, color measurement, color literature, color-space design, visual communications, lighting design and ergonomics, perceptual psychology, media and materials, computer studies, and humanities.

Students study existing buildings and create color schemes for building facades in downtown Helsinki, Finland. (Photo: Harald Arnkil, Department of Art, UIAH.)

Color Design Research Unit, South Bank University, London

Color is where art and science meet. To help industries of every kind, color science has developed sophisticated electronic tools, taking the guesswork out of color specification. The fusion of ideas and information about color may develop new and unique products, leading to increased sales and profitability.

The Color Design Research Unit of South Bank University in London, England, offers color training programs in color consultancy and research related directly to the field of color marketing, product development, and design. Studying under experts in a variety of fields (e.g., color trends in food, durable products, clothing and textiles; the psychology of color; packaging and paint), students with an interest in color and marketing will find many opportunities to further their education and explore both in short-course certificate programs and also new postgraduate and research programs currently in planning.

The Color Design Research Unit is supported by a fully equipped studio. The research involves a continuing study of trends in consumer preferences and color application. The unit also advises industry on which colors to use in product color ranges, forecasts color trends, and helps manufacturers use color as a marketing tool. These services may involve the preparation of reports, research, or advising on selling with color.

The recognized importance of color as an economical yet effective tool in the field of product development, and an essential part of the marketing process, prompted the establishment of the Color Design Research Unit to meet the needs of these industries. The unit operates across a wide range of product sectors, developing color solutions for today's highly design-conscious environment, and providing training, development, and related consultancy services designed to improve competitiveness.

The key objectives of the unit include:

- To provide a focus for the industrial and commercial application of color research in design, manufacturing, marketing, and retailing today
- To increase the transfer of technology and design skills in the development of technical and analytical aspects of color usage
- To encourage investment in color design development, application, and management
- To develop the use of color technology within industry through the provision of consultancy services

The Color Design Research Unit is located at South Bank University, 103 Borough Road, London SE1 0AA, UK.

International Association of Color Consultants/Designers

In 1957, with the participation of authorities on architecture, design, color science, and art from 12 countries, the International Association of Color Consultants (IACC) was founded in Holland. Facing an acute shortage of professional consultants and an absence of possibilities for competent training in the field, the first elected IACC president, Dr. Heinrich Frieling, director and founder of the Institute for Color Psychology nine years earlier, was instructed to establish and direct an educational program known as the IACC Seminars.

These seminars trained students to be color consultants. The seminars were (and are today) recognized for their comprehensive, interdisciplinary approach to all areas connected with color: physics, psychology, light technology, physiology, biology, visual ergonomics, aesthetics, art, philosophy, and professionalism. The presence of the first-class lectures and the international array of IACC vice presidents, many of them from the architectural field, ensured that the IACC Color Consultant/Designer Diploma would be a testimony to intensive training. Professional accreditation is also given by the European Association of Color Consultants of the IACC to professionals (e.g., architects, interior architects, designers) who pass IACC standards without necessarily having graduated from the IACC Seminars. In the United States this is not the case: The North American Association of Color Consultants/ Designers (NAACC) of the IACC only accepts IACC-graduated individuals.

Today, worldwide interest is shown in the IACC training program and accreditation, reflecting a growing awareness of the necessity for the profession and its standards.

Frank H. Mahnke, president of the IACC, oversees a highly effective and professional education curriculum. The core curriculum of the IACC Seminars for Color and Environment consists of six obligatory seminars, each six days in length, conducted twice a year for three years. (The IACC seminars in the United States are somewhat more condensed and shorter than those in Europe.) Home assignments are given during the time the seminars are not in session. Additional days are included for the presentation/review of assignments/projects and examinations. IACC seminars in Europe also offer nonobligatory one- to two-day seminars that are not a requirement for the IACC Diploma.

Obligatory Seminars:

Seminar 1: Color Phenomena
- Introduction into the IACC philosophy
- Introduction into color
- Introduction into psychological and physiological aspects of color
- Fundamentals of vision
- Color as phenomenon, reality, and experience (subjective/objective)
- Goethe and the color sciences
- Creativity and artistic self-experience
- Fundamentals of material/products and techniques of use

Seminar 2: Light/Color/Human Beings
- Physical and psycho-physiological aspects of light

- Fundamentals of illuminating engineering
- Illuminating the architectural space
- Biological effects of light (health, mood, behavior)
- Dramaturgical design with light and color
- Materials/products and techniques of use

Seminar 3: Visual Communication/Color as Information

- Syntax, pragmatism, and semantics as criteria for quality control of color designs
- Psychology of color perception
- Color as information in advertising/marketing
- Color/form relationships in advertising/marketing
- Information content of color design in the architectural space
- Symbolizing/visualizing
- Color as an information medium
- Information/manipulation

Seminar 4: Humans/Color/Architectural Space

- Perceiving and responding to the architectural space (room experience and behavior)
- Human response to color and the environment
- Systematic color design of workplaces, schools, kindergartens/preschools, medical and psychiatric hospitals, and old-age/retirement homes

Seminar 5: Systemized and Systematic Design

- Systematic color planning for creative and human-oriented environmental design
- Color systems—their development, limits, and possibilities
- Pigments and painting techniques from historical times to today
- Project design—from conception to implementation

- Possibilities of color design presentation on CADs

Seminar 6: Color and Environment
- Synesthetic architecture
- Color design in anthropological philosophy
- Baubiologie (building biology)
- Color in townscape—past, present, and future
- Project townscape color design
- Summary of the psychological and physiological aspects of color design (of all six seminars)

Additional, Nonobligatory Seminars

(duration: one to two days, before or after an obligatory seminar)

- Design Practice
- Color Psychology in Depth
- Artistic Expression
- Psychology of the Architectural Space
- Painting and Mixing Techniques at the Project Site
- Self-Management—Competently Representing Yourself

In the United States the IACC conducts a special IACC Accreditation/Qualification Seminar for interior design graduates of Brigham Young University who have taken the postgraduate course "Advanced Color," which is based on the IACC professional philosophy and professional standards.

IACC also conducts a non-IACC accreditation introductory seminar at the Center for Architectural Construction and Environment, Donau University, Krems, Austria.

Color/space facade. This six-step progressive color design project at Lawrence Technological University begins with an example of an entryway and culminates in color studies which act to enhance and then camouflage the dimensional aspects of form. The final stage, in three dimensions, explores color and form in the round and their dynamic attributes of spatial enhancement. (Project: Gail M. Bruner. Photo: Gretchen Rudy.)

Environmental Color Design at Lawrence Technological University

"Environmental Color Design" at Lawrence Technological University's College of Architecture and Design in Southfield, Michigan, is an advanced course for students of architecture, interior design, and illustration who wish to take on a "real-world" color design project based on an existing problem in urban design, architecture, and environmental design. Lawrence Technological University recently established advanced coursework in the area of color related to the architectural environment to promote a visual and realistic understanding of the qualities of building materials and their potential for aesthetic design statements. All students in the design program at Lawrence receive color study content in the foundation program common to all

Final stage of color/space facade. Color is explored as interrelated to the enhancement and camouflage of a three-dimensional construction in the round. (Project: Gail M. Bruner. Photo: Gretchen Rudy.)

undergraduate majors. The following student project in color and three-dimensional planning is typical of the nature of first-year color studio work. Beyond this beginning exposure, the Environmental Color Design course has undertaken a realistic project for the color design of new apartment buildings planned in Helsinki, Finland, in the area known as Ruoholahti Harbor. Students had the opportunity to speak with an architect from the city planning office and to work with documentation and abundant visual resources regarding the history and development of the city and harbor area. They also used color research information, on-site materials, and

Student project from the advanced
Environmental Color Design course at Lawrence
Technological University, in collaboration with the
City Planning Office of Helsinki, Finland. Color
schemes for the facades, street furnishings, and
shoreline of new apartment buildings planned for
Ruoholahti Harbor in downtown Helsinki,
Finland. (Project: Stephen D. Landon. Photo:
Harold Linton.)

colors created in Helsinki and brought back for
the project by Professor Linton. The illustrations
depict two of several works that were created in
the Environmental Color Design studio and later
exhibited in the gallery of the city planning
offices of Helsinki. The design objectives were to
take a new look at this highly visible point of
entry from the sea to Helsinki and to provide the
city architects with inspiration and fresh opinions
about facade and color design for the harbor
development area.

In addition to these experiences, the college
offers information on a variety of topics related

to color education opportunities, color for architecture and allied design professions, and color
research related to industry and the design environment. The College of Architecture and
Design at Lawrence Technological University is
one of the largest architectural programs in the
United States, with undergraduate and graduate
degree programs in architecture, interior archi-
tecture/design, and architectural illustration.
Professor Harold Linton, assistant dean, is a
principal instructor of advanced courses in color
design and serves as a consultant to industry on
problems related to color and design and to
those seeking technical information regarding
the role of color performance and materials.

*Student project from the advanced Environmental
Color Design course at Lawrence Technological
University, in collaboration with the City Planning
Office of Helsinki, Finland. Color schemes for the
facades, street furnishings, and shoreline of new
apartment buildings planned for Ruoholahti
Harbor in downtown Helsinki, Finland. (Project:
Steven Collins. Photo: Harold Linton.)*

References

1. Oberascher, L. The language of colour. In: A. Niemcsis and J. Schanda (eds.), *AIC—Color 93, Proceeding of the 7th Congress of the International Colour Association,* vol. A. Budapest, Technical University of Budapest (1993): 188/1–4.

2. Schreibmayr, P. On truth in size. In: B. Martens (ed.): Full-scale modeling in the age of virtual reality, *Proceedings of the 6th European Full-scale Modeling Association Conference in Vienna.* Wien: RIS-ISIS Publications at OKK Editions, vol. 2. Osterreichischer Kunst- und Kulturverlag (1996): 35.

3. Swedish Standards Institution. 1979. SS 01 00 *Colour Notation System,* SIS.

4. Caivano, J. Cesia: A system of visual signs complementing color. *Color Research and Application,* 12 (1991): 258–268.

5. Caivano, J. Appearance (cesia): Constructing of scales by means of spinning disks. *Color Research and Application,* 19 (1994): 351–362.

6. Green-Armytage, P. Beyond colour. In: A. Niemcsis and J. Schanda (eds.), *AIC—Color 93, Proceeding of the 7th Congress of the International Colour Association,* vol. A. Budapest, Technical University of Budapest (1993): 22/1–8.

7. Oberascher, L. Die sprache der farbe. Trendfarben, individualität, motivation. In: *DBZ Deutsche Bauzeitschrift, Sondemummer,* Buro 1991. Gutersloh: Bertelsmann (1991): 88–97.

8. Hutchings, J. The continuity of colour, design, art, and science. I. The philosophy of the total appearance concept and image measurement. *Color Research and Application,* 20 (1995): 296–306.

9. Hutchings, J. The continuity of colour, design, art, and science. II. Application of the total appear-

ance concept to image creation. *Color Research and Application,* 20 (1995): 307–312.

10. Craik, K. H., Feimer, N. R. 1989. Environmental assessment. In: Altman, D., Stokols, I., *Handbook of Environmental Psychology,* New York: John Wiley & Sons, 891–918.

11. Bosselmann, P., Craik, K. H. 1987. Perceptual simulations of environments. In: R. B. Bechtel, R. W. Marans, W. Michelson (eds.), *Methods in Environmental and Behavioral Research.* New York: Van Nostrand Reinhold, 162–190.

12. Martens, B. 1995. *Raumliche Simulationstechniken in der Architektur.* Europaische Hochschulschriften, Reihe 37, Architektur, Bd. 14. Frankfurt am Main: Peter Lang.

13. Schonberger, A. Architekturmodelle zwischen illusion and simulation. In: A. Schonberger (Hrsg.), *Simulation und Wirkichkeit.* Köln: DuMont Buchverlag (1988), 41–54.

14. Schawelka, K. 1993. Bemerkungen zum farbigen architekturentwurf um 1800. Unveröffentlichtes Manuskript.

15. Martens, B. "Finishing Touch" für das Raumexperimentierlabor an der Technischen Universität Wien. Bauforum, 165 (1994): 52–57.

APPENDIX A

Color Order Systems and Tools

Munsell Color: The Universal Language

The Munsell System of Color Notation is the universal system for selecting, communicating, identifying, and controlling color.

At the beginning of the twentieth century, Albert H. Munsell revolutionized the world of color communication. Where vague nomenclature and even conflicting descriptions had been the norm, Munsell established an orderly system for accurately identifying every color that exists. His idea was so simple and so practical that today the Munsell System of Color Notation is established and recognized as the standard for color notation throughout the world.

Munsell's Idea

Munsell developed the three-dimensional concept of color. He called these three dimensions or attributes of color *hue, value,* and *chroma.* In the color space Munsell conceived, five principal hues are arranged in a circle, from red to yellow to green to blue to purple and back to red. Between these, he named five intermediate colors: yellow-red, green-yellow, blue-green, purple-blue, and red-purple. These ten hues are placed equidistant from one another around the circumference of the circle, blending one into another.

In Munsell color space, a value scale forms the vertical axis. The scale of values ranges from 0 for pure black to 10 for pure white. Black, white, and the grays between them are called neutral colors, because they have no hue. Colors that have hue are called chromatic colors. The value scale applies to chromatic colors as well as to neutral colors.

Chroma extends horizontally from the neutral axis in Munsell color space. Black, grays, and white have 0 chroma. Chroma increases outward from the center of color space, representing an increase in color saturation or intensity.

With the Munsell System of Color Notation, any color can be identified by its hue, value, and chroma. Each of these attributes is independent of the others, and one may be varied without affecting the other two. However, the omission of one of these attributes would leave us in doubt as to the character of a color. It is like trying to communicate the size of a room without having all three of its measurements.

Chroma is the strength of a color. It is the quality by which we distinguish a strong color (as, for example, distinguishing a dull green from a vivid green).

Hue is that quality by which we distinguish one color family from another (as red from yellow, or blue from green).

Value is the quality by which we distinguish a light color from a dark one.

The exact Munsell notation of a color sample may be ascertained through visually comparing it to the chips in a Munsell Book of Color, or by measuring the color with a spectrophotometer and then converting the data on a computer. Being able to utilize the Munsell System in both visual and instrumental applications is one of the unique benefits it affords.

Color Communications

Precise representations of the colors from the Munsell System are available in books and in swatches of various sizes, in matte and glossy finishes. They make it easy to specify and communicate exact color selections to anyone, anywhere, and are used worldwide in industry, art, and science.

Educational Materials

Teaching aids and instructional materials from Munsell are used in schools and on the job. They make the complexities of color understandable by giving color appearance and color relationships a logical order and common language.

Custom Color Services

Munsell offers custom color services to help establish the standards and tolerances for any color you specify for your products, logos, and packaging. Standards for gloss and texture can also be established. Standards can be created from a sample, a numerical specification, or an idea.

Specialty Color Charts

Unique color reference materials produced by Munsell play a vital role in many industrial and scientific fields. Soil charts, wire coding charts, and photo, film, and video color aids are examples. Munsell will develop color charts to meet any special application.

Color Vision Tests

Munsell provides special color vision tests in industries where visual color discrimination is important, as well as for medical and psychological testing.

Color-Eye 7000 Spectrophotometer by GretagMacbeth™

The nature of color measurement in industry and the importance of accuracy of color judgment across the spectrum of product manufacturing requires highly sophisticated instruments such as a spectrophotometer to measure a variety of product materials and opaque to translucent color surfaces. The Color-Eye 7000 Spectrophotometer is the instrument of choice for dedicated color analysis in either a laboratory or a manufacturing setting. Measurements from samples are translated into stored numerical standards for later comparison to related materials and colors. Products which pass manufacturers' outgoing color inspections must also pass customers' incoming color inspections.

Combined with appropriate computer hardware and Macbeth color control or color formulation software, the Color-Eye 7000 is ideal for the color laboratory, research facility, and highly demanding manufacturing sites. The enhanced numerical precision delineates steep-slope, high-chroma colors for reflectance samples as well as transmission samples, from the transparent to the translucent.

Color-Eye 7000 Spectrophotometer by Gretag-Macbeth™. (Courtesy of GretagMacbeth.)

SpectraLight® II Color Viewing System by GretagMacbeth™

The GretagMacbeth SpectraLight® II has a visual color evaluation system used in quality control laboratories and manufacturing sites for accurate, visual evaluation of color materials and products. It provides an "A" rating when evaluated using the CIE assessment method of daylight simulators as specified in CIE Publication #51. SpectraLight II handles critical color evaluations by providing the most accurate simulation of daylight available today. This daylight accu-

SpectraLight®II Color Viewing System by GretagMacbeth™. (Courtesy of Gretag-Macbeth.)

racy is achieved by utilizing patented filtered tungsten halogen technology, in which light from a continuous tungsten halogen source is passed through proprietary GretagMacbeth filters. When the ultraviolet source is activated with the daylight source, it provides near UV energy in the same proportion found in natural daylight.

The Natural Color System (NCS)

The NCS Natural Color System is a logical color system which builds on how the human being

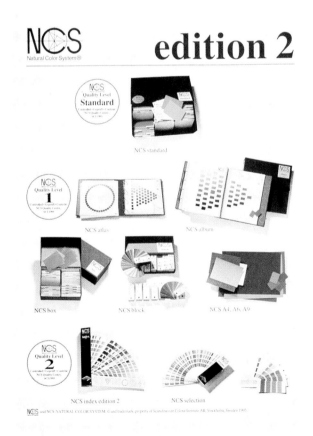

Various NCS color system products useful for studio and industry practice. (NCS—Natural Color System, © and trademark, property of the Scandinavian Colour Institute AB, Stockholm, Sweden.)

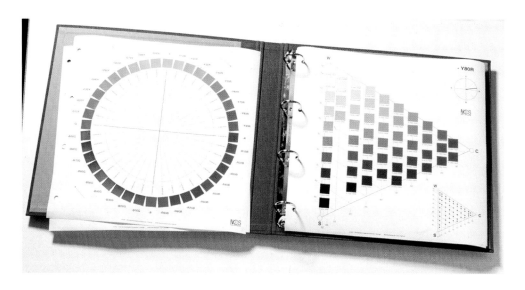

The Natural Color System (NCS) Atlas demonstrates the organization of the color system. (Courtesy of the Scandinavian Colour Institute AB, Stockholm, Sweden.)

sees color. With NCS, all imaginable surface colors can be described and given unambiguous NCS notations.

The six pure or elementary colors which are the basis of the built-in ability of humans to characterize different colors are white (W), black (S), yellow (Y), red (R), blue (B), and green (G). NCS color notations are based on how much a given color seems to resemble these six elementary colors.

In the NCS designation 2030-Y90R, for example, 2030 indicates the nuance (i.e., the degree of resemblance to black S and to the maximum hue C); in this case, 20 percent blackness and 30 percent chromaticness. The hue Y90R indicates the percentage resemblance of the color to two chromatic elementary colors, here Y and R. Y90R means yellow with 90 percent redness.

Purely gray colors lack color hue and are only given nuance notations followed by N (as neutral). 0500-N is white, and this is followed by 1000-N, 1500-N, 2000-N, and so on to 9000-N, which is black.

A letter S preceding the complete NCS notation (as in S 2030-Y90R) means that the NCS sample is from the second edition.

APPENDIX B

International Color Organizations

The following is a list of color organizations, arranged alphabetically by country name:

Grupo Argentiono del Color Lic.
R. D. Lozano
INTI Division Opica
Cas de Correo 157
1650 San Martin Buenos Aires
Argentina

Colour Society of Australia
Dr. B. Powell
P.O. Box E 184
St James
NSW 2000
Australia

Arbeitskreis Farbe der Ove-Olav
Dr. F. Rotter
Fachgruppe Messtechnik
Arltgasse 35
A-1163 Wien
Austria

Centre D'Information de la Couleur Belgique
Mme. J. Verschueren van Hedden
S. A. Levis N.V.
171 Leuvensesteenweh
B-1800 Vilvoorde
Belgium

Canadian Society for Color
Dr. A. R. Robertson
National Research Council
Division Physics
Ottawa K1A 0R6
Canada

Chinese Colour Commission
Prof. Shu Yuexin
Shandong Textile Engineering College
Dept. of Colour Science
Qingdao
China

Centre Francais de la Couleur
Dr. Robert Seve
15 passage de la Main d'Or
75011 Paris
France

Deutscher Vervand Farbe
Dr. G. Geutler
Institute for Lichttechnik, TU
Einsteinufer 19
D-1000 Berlin 10
Germany

The Color Group
Dr. M. R. Pointer
Kodak Ltd., Res. Div.
Headstone Drive
Harrow, Middlesex HA1 4TY
Great Britain

Nederlandse Vereniging Voor Kleurenstudie
Dr. C. H. Kleemans
Zuidlaan 22
NL-211 GC Aerdenhout
Holland

Hungarian National Colour Committee
Dr. A. Niemcsisc
Technical University of Budapest
Muegyetem rkp. 3
H-1111 Budapest
Hungary

Colour Group of India
Dr. N. S. Gangakhedkar
Compute Spectra Pvt. Ltd.
1, Manisha Malviya Road
Vile Parle (E)
Bombay 400 057
India

Associazione Ottica Italiana
Prof. L. R. Ronchi
Instituto Nazionale di Ottica
6 Largo Fermi
1-50125 Firenza
Italy

Color Planning Center, Inc.
7-6 Bakurocho Chome Nihonbashi
Chuo-Ku
Tokyo 103
Japan

Color Science Association of Japan
A. Kodama
Japan Color Research Institute
1-19 Nishiazabuy 3 Ch.
Minato-Qu
Tokyo 106
Japan

Norsk Farveforum
U. Willumsen
P.O. Box 1714 Hystad
N-3200 Sandefjord
Norway

Polish Committee for Standardization
Prof. Dr. Sobczak
ul. Elektroralna 2
PL-139 Warzawa
Poland

South African Colour Science Association
A. N. Chalmers
P.O. Box 36319
Menlo Park
Pretoria 0102
South Africa

Svenska Fareggruppen
Th. Hord
Swedish Colour Centre Foundation
P.O. Box 14038
S-10440 Stockholm
Sweden

International Association of Color
    Consultants
Frank Mahnke
11 Quai Capo d'Istria
Geneva 1205
Switzerland

Schweizerische Lichttenchnishe Geselschaft
A. O. Wuillemin
Postfach
Ch-8034 Zurich
Switzerland

American Association of Textile Chemists and
    Colorists
William R. Martin
P.O. Box 12215
Research Triangle Park, NC 27709
United States

American Information Center for Color and
    Environment
Erna Haynes
3621 Alexia Place
San Diego, CA 92116
United States

Color Association of the United States
Dolores Ware
343 Lexington Avenue
New York, NY 10016
United States

Color Education Center
Professor Harold Linton
College of Architecture and Design
Lawrence Technological University
21000 W. Ten Mile Road
Southfield, MI 48075
United States

Color Marketing Group
Nancy Burns
4001 North Ninth Street
Suite 102
Arlington, VA 22203
United States

Dry Color Manufacturers Association
J. L. Robinson
206 N. Washington Street
Alexandria, VA 22320-1839
United States

International Association of Color
    Consultants
Rudolf Mahnke
730 Pennsylvania Avenue
San Diego, CA 92103
United States

Inter-Society Color Council
Mrs. Joy Turner Luke
Studio 231
Box 18, Route 1
Sperryville, VA 22740
United States

National Paint and Coatings
    Association, Inc.
Larry L. Thomas
1500 Rhode Island Avenue, NW
Washington, DC 20005
United States

CREDITS

Part I

Color Designer: Eva Fay, Rushcutters Bay, Australia. Photographers: Tony Gunn, Russell Brooks, Patrick Bingham-Hall, and *Australian House and Garden*. Architects: Walton & Associates, Kerry McGrath.

Architect and Landscape and Color Designer: Malvina Arrarte Grau, Lima, Peru.

Color Designer: Jean-Philippe Lenclos, Atelier 3d Couleur, Paris, France.

Part II

Color Designer: Donald Kaufman Color, New York, New York. Architects: Kuwabara Payne McKenna Blumburg, Toronto, Ontario, Canada. Photographer: Steven Evans.

Architect: Shashi Caan, Associate, Gensler & Associates, New York, New York. Photographer: P. Ennis. Structural Engineer: Cantor Seinuk Group, New York, New York. Mechanical/Electrical: Edwards & Zuck, P.E., New York, New York. General Contractor: Lehr Construction Corp., New York, New York. Lighting: HDA Lighting Design, New York, New York. Project Team: Principal, Walter A. Hunt Jr.; Director, Robin Klehr Avia; Architect/Manager, Gregory A. Shunick; Designer, Shashi B. Caan; Architect, Kavita Dhir-Mallik; CAAD Operator, Hau T. Hsu; Client, Fidelity Investments.

Interior Designer: Begona Munoz, Principado de Asturias.

Interior Designer: Lynn Augstein, ASID CID, Sausalito,
California. Photographer: Douglas A. Salin. Con-
tractor: Bo Potts, J.T. Construction, San Anselmo,
California. Painter: Lance Phillips, Rhonert Park,
California. Tile: Mike Schubert, MLS Tile, Peta-
luma, California. Designers: Shawn Hunt, Sausalito,
California; Rick Sambol, Novato, California.

Part III

Architect: Perry Dean Rogers & Partners, Boston,
Massachusetts. Author, Color and Context:
Michael J. Crosbie. Anne Johnson, Marketing
Manager, United States Embassy, Amman, Jordan.
Designer: Deborah Sussman, Sussman/Prejza & Com-
pany, Inc. Architect: Barton Myers Associates. Proj-
ect Design Team: Deborah Sussman, Charles
Milhaupt. Painter: Vomar. Photographer: Tim Grif-
fith.
Color Designer: Lourdes Legorreta, Legorreta Arqui-
tectos, Palacio de Versalles, Mexico. Architect:
Ricardo Legorreta, Victor Legorreta, Noe Castro,
Legorreta Arquitectos. Design Team: Miguel
Almaraz, Gerardo Alonso, Benjamin Gonzalez.
Landscape Design: James Cooper. Architect of
Record: Johnson-Dempsey & Associates. Associate
Architect: Davis Sprinkle & Robey Architects. Proj-
ect Management: 3D International. Interior Design:
Ford, Powell & Carson/Humberto Saldana/Callins
& Associates. Structural Design: Danish-Lundy Pin-
nel. MEP Engineer: Goetting & Associates. Artists:
Stephen Antanakos (Neon Light), Jesse Trevino
(Mural). Contractor: H. A. Lott, Inc. Photographer:
Lourdes Legorreta and Paul Bardajgy.
Gerald Reinbold, Vice President, SHG Incorporated,
Detroit, Michigan.
John Outram, Principal, John Outram Associates,
Architects, London, England.

Part IV

Gere Kavanaugh/Designs, Los Angeles, California.

CZWG Architects, London, England.

Tomas Taveira, Lisbon, Portugal.

Stephen Donald, Architects Limited, Madigan + Donald Architects, London, England.

Colorist: Jorma Hautala, Helsinki, Finland. Architect: Juhani Pallasmaa, Helsinki, Finland.

Design Etc., New York, New York. KNEX Showroom, New York, New York. Donald Campbell & Trench Bradey, Designers.

Elke Arora, Interior Designer, Hannover, Germany.

Part V

Judith Ruttenberg, Architects, Color Designer & Consultant, Ramat-gan, Israel.

Jean-Philippe Lenclos, Atelier 3d Couleur, Paris, France.

Part VI

Shingo Yoshida, Color Planning Center, Tokyo, Japan.

Michael Lancaster, Architect, Landscape Architect & Color Consultant, London, England.

Giovanni Brino, Architect, Torino, Italy.

Part VII

Sculpture: Brian Clarke, London, England.

Sculptor: Charles Ross, New York, New York. Concept: Virginia Dwan. Architect: Laban Wingert. United World College, New Mexico.

Artist: Harold Linton. Color Consultant: Eugene R. Baker. Interior Designer: Stuart Fine, Architect. Temple Israel, W. Bloomfield, Michigan.

Part VIII

Paul Urbanek, Architect. Harley Ellington Design, Southfield, Michigan. 3M Corporation, Livonia, Michigan.

Donna Cox, Professor, School of Art and Design, University of Illinois, Urbana-Champaign.

Dr. Leonhard Oberascher, Institute fur Angewandte Okologische Psychologie, Salzburg, Austria. Akzo Nobel/Sikkens Ges. m.b.H., Phillips Licht GmbH, M. Kaind/Kronospan, Leube Baustoffe, for their assistance in realizing the full-scale models.

Leonhard Oberascher. The language of colour. In: A. Niemcsis and J. Schanda (eds.): *AIC—Color 93, Proceedings of the 7th Congress of the International Colour Association*, vol. A. Budapest, Technical University of Budapest (1993) 188/1–4.

P. Schreibmayr. On truth in size. In: B. Martens (ed.): Full-scale modeling in the age of virtual reality, *Proceedings of the 6th European Full-scale Modeling Association Conference in Vienna.* Wien: RIS-ISIS Publications at OKK Editions, vol. 2. Osterreichischer Kunst- und Kulturverlag (1996) 35.

Swedish Standards Institution. 1979 SS 01 00 *Colour Notation System*, SIS.

J. Caivano. Cesia: A system of visual signs complementing color. *Color Research and Application*, 12 (1991) 258–268.

———— Appearance (cesia): Constructing of scales by means of spinning disks. *Color Research and Application*, 19 (1994) 351–362.

P. Green-Armytage. Beyond colour. In: A. Niemcsis and J. Schanda (eds.): *AIC—COLOR 93, Proceedings of the 7th Congress of the International Colour Association*, vol. A. Budapest, Technical University of Budapest (1993) 22/1–8.

Leonhard Oberascher. Die sprache der farbe. Trendfarben, individualitat, motivation. In: *DBZ*

Deutsche Bauzeitschrift, Sondemummer: Buro 1991. Gutersloh: Bertelsmann (1991) 88–97.

J. Hutchings. The continuity of colour, design, art, and science. II. Application of the total appearance concept to image creation. *Color Research and Application,* 20 (1995) 307–312.

K. H. Craik and N. R. Feimer. Environmental assessment. In: D. Altman and L. Stokols: *Handbook of Environmental Psychology,* New York: John Wiley & Sons (1989) 891–918.

P. Bosselmann and K. H. Craik. Perceptual simulations of environments. In: R. B. Bechtel, R. W. Marans, and W. Michelson (eds.): *Methods in Environmental and Behavioral Research.* New York: Van Nostrand Reinhold (1987) 162–190.

B. Martens. 1995. *Raumliche Simulationstechniken in der Architektur.* Europaische Hochschulschriften, Reihe 37, Architektur, Bd. 14. Frankfurt am Main: Peter Lang.

A. Schonberger. Architekturmodelle zwischen illusion and simulation. In: A. Schonberger (Hrsg.): *Simulation und Wirkichkeit.* Köln: DuMont Buchverlag (1988) 41–54.

K. Schawelka Bemerkungen zum farbigen architekturentwurf um 1800. Unveroffentlichtes manuskript.

B. Martens "Finishing Touch" für das Raumexperimentierlabor an der Technischen Universitat Wien. Bauforum, 165 (1994) 52–57.

Harald Arnkil, Senior Lecturer of Art, The University of Art and Design, UIAH, Helsinki, Finland. Sakari Marila, Chairman, Department of Art and Design, UIAH, Helsinki, Finland.

Hilary Dalke, Director, Colour Design Research Unit, South Bank University, London, England.

Frank Mahnke, President, International Association of Color Consultants/Designers, San Diego, California.

Gretchen Rudy, Lecturer, College of Architecture and Design, Lawrence Technological University, Southfield, Michigan.

Center for Color Education, College of Architecture and Design, Lawrence Technological University, Southfield, Michigan.

Appendix A

Elaine Tito, GretagMacbeth, New Windsor, New York.

Cathy Hofknecht, Marketing Manager, Gretag-Macbeth.

Berit Bergstrom, Director, Color Education, Scandinavian Color Institute AB, Stockholm, Sweden.

BIBLIOGRAPHY

Albers, Josef. *The Interaction of Color.* New Haven,
 Conn.: Yale University Press, 1963.

Arnheim, Rudolf. *Art and Visual Perception.* Berkeley,
 Calif.: University of California Press, 1954.

Arnkil, Harald, and Esa Hamalainen. *Aspects of
 Color.* Helsinki, Finland: University of Art and
 Design, Helsinki UIAH, 1995.

Birren, Faber. *History of Color in Painting.* New York:
 Van Nostrand Reinhold, 1965.

———. *Light, Color and Environment.* Rev. ed. New
 York: Van Nostrand Reinhold, 1982.

Duttman J., and J. Uhl. *Color in Townscape.* Translated from German by John William Bagriel. San
 Francisco: W. H. Freeman and Company, 1981.

Eiseman, Leatrice. *Alive with Color.* Reston, Va.:
 Acropolis Books, 1983.

Eiseman, Leatrice, and Lawrence Herbert. *The Pan-
 tone Book of Color.* New York: Harry N. Abrams,
 Inc., 1990.

Ellinger, Richard G. *Color Structure and Design.* New
 York: Van Nostrand Reinhold, 1980.

Favre, Jean-Paul, and Andre November. *Color and
 Communication.* Zurich, Switzerland: ABC Verlag,
 1979.

Gerritsen, Frans. *Theory and Practice of Color.* New
 York: Van Nostrand Reinhold, 1975.

Hope, Augustine, and Margaret Walch. *The Color
 Compendium.* New York: Van Nostrand Reinhold,
 1990.

Itten, Johannes. *The Art of Color.* New York: Van
 Nostrand Reinhold, 1973.

Kaufman, Donald, and Taffy Dahl. *Color: Natural
 Palettes for Painted Rooms.* New York: Clarkson N.
 Potter, Inc., 1992.

Kavanaugh, Gere. "Color Library." *Interior Design* (August 1988): 206.

Kubler, George. *The Shape of Time.* New Haven, Conn.: Yale University Press, 1962.

Lam, William. *Perception and Lighting as Formgivers for Architecture.* New York: McGraw-Hill, 1977.

Lancaster, Michael. *Colourscape.* London: Academy Editions, 1996.

Lenclos, Jean-Philippe, and Dominique Lenclos. *The Colors of France: Architecture and Landscape.* Paris: Moniteur, 1982.

———. *Les Couleurs De L'Europe: Geographic De La Couleur.* Paris: Publications du Moniteur, 1995.

Libby, William Charles. *Color and the Structural Sense.* Englewood Cliffs, N.J.: Prentice-Hall, Inc., 1974.

Linton, Harold. *Color Model Environments.* New York: Van Nostrand Reinhold, 1985.

———. *Color Consulting: A Survey of International Color Design.* New York: Van Nostrand Reinhold, 1991.

———. *Color Forecasting: A Survey of International Color Marketing.* New York: Van Nostrand Reinhold, 1994.

Mahnke, Frank H. *Color, Environment and Human Response.* New York: Van Nostrand Reinhold (ITP), 1996.

Michel, Lou. *Light: The Shape of Space.* New York: Van Nostrand Reinhold, 1996.

Miller, Mary C. *Color for Interior Architecture.* New York: John Wiley & Sons, Inc., 1997.

Moholy-Hagy, Laszlo. *Vision in Motion.* Chicago: Hillison and Etten Company, 1947.

Munsell, A. H. *A Color Notation.* 12th ed. Baltimore: Munsell Color Company, 1975.

Norman, Richard B. *Electronic Color.* New York: Van Nostrand Reinhold, 1969.

Ostwald, Wilhelm. *The Color Primer.* New York: Van Nostrand Reinhold, 1969.

Porter, Tom. *How Architects Visualize.* New York: Van Nostrand Reinhold, 1979.

———. *Architectural Color: A Design Guide to Using Color on Buildings.* New York: The Whitney Library of Design, 1982.

Porter, Tom, and Byron Mikellides. *Color for Architecture.* New York: Van Nostrand Reinhold, 1976.

Rochon, Richard, and Harold Linton. *Color in Architectural Illustration.* New York: Van Nostrand Reinhold, 1989.

Rotzler, Willy. *Constructive Concepts: A History of Constructive Art from Cubism to the Present.* New York: Rizzoli International Publications, Inc., 1977.

Sloane, Patricia. *Primary Sources: Selected Writings on Color from Aristotle to Albers.* New York: Design Press, 1991.

Smith, Charles N. *Student Handbook of Color.* New York: Van Nostrand Reinhold. 1965.

Swirnoff, Lois. *Dimensional Color.* Boston: Birkhauser Boston, Inc., 1989.

Toy, Maggie (ed.). *Architectural Design: Colour in Architecture.* London: Academy Group Ltd., 1996.

Varley, H. (ed.). *Color.* London: Marshall Editions Limited, 1980.

Walch, Margaret, and Augustine Hope. *Living Colors: The Definitive Guide to Color Palettes Through the Ages.* New York: Chronicle Books, 1995.

INDEX

About the Author

Professor Harold Linton is recognized as one of the world's foremost experts in architectural color theory and application. He is currently Chairman of the Department of Art at Bradley University in Peoria, Illinois, and the former Assistant Dean of the College of Architecture and Design of Lawrence Technological University in Southfield, Michigan. He initiated the first BFA program in Architectural Illustration in the United States, and coestablished the first European graduate program in Color Studies at the University of Art and Design in Helsinki, Finland. Among his many written works is the best-selling text *Portfolio Design*, as well as *Color Forecasting*, *Color Consulting*, *Sketching the Concept*, *Architectural Sketching in Markers*, *Color in Architectural Illustration*, and *Color Model Environments*.